P9-CIS-204

FAT GIRL *Walking* ⇶⟶

DEY ST.

AN IMPRINT OF
WILLIAM MORROW PUBLISHERS

FAT GIRL
Walking

SEX, FOOD, LOVE *AND*

Being Comfortable in Your Skin . . .
Every Inch of It

Brittany Gibbons

DEY ST.

The names and identifying characteristics of most of the individuals throughout this book have been changed to protect their privacy.

FAT GIRL WALKING. Copyright © 2015 by Brittany Gibbons. All rights reserved. Printed in the United States of America. No part of this book may be used or reproduced in any manner whatsoever without written permission except in the case of brief quotations embodied in critical articles and reviews. For information address HarperCollins Publishers, 195 Broadway, New York, NY 10007.

HarperCollins books may be purchased for educational, business, or sales promotional use. For information please e-mail the Special Markets Department at SPsales@harpercollins.com.

FIRST EDITION

Designed by Paula Russell Szafranski

Library of Congress Cataloging-in-Publication Data has been applied for.

ISBN 978-06-234303-1

15 16 17 18 19 OV/RRD 10 9 8 7 6 5 4 3 2 1

Dedication TK

CONTENTS

INTRODUCTION

"OKAY, BRITTANY, NOW if you could just walk out in your bikini and pretend you're just a normal woman wearing a bathing suit?"

"I *am* a normal woman wearing a bathing suit," I said.

"Right, right. So we're going to pan the camera up, guys if you could go slower when we get to her stretch marks and chest, and Brittany, if you could just smile and act happy during all of this, that'd be great."

"Smile and act happy while you pan the camera across my stretch marks. Got it."

I stood on the cement patio of our rented vacation house in Orlando, while three men from *Good Morning America* adjusted lighting and discussed the best way to showcase the anomaly that was a chubby girl in a bikini. I glanced up at my publicist, Jackie, who sat behind the camera. She smiled and gave me the thumbs-up, and suddenly Monty Python's "Galaxy Song" played in my head and I smiled as it hit me.

So remember, when you're feeling very small and insecure

I am the Internet's token fat girl. If the Internet is still a thing when I am old and die, all this might be included in my obituary.

Brittany Gibbons: the jolly face of plus-size women. Known for taking her clothes off to make political statements and making skinny people everywhere uncomfortable.

Growing up, I had reoccurring daydreams about one day being famous, marrying Dr. Peter Venkman from *Ghostbusters,* and writing lots of books. I never planned to be Internet famous, which is a totally different kind of famous, by the way.

You see, there are lots of ways to be Internet famous, like being adorable British girls in tutus who rap, eating cups of feces with your best friend, or being absolutely any kind of cat. But for me, the keys to my success are just being not slim, making vagina jokes on social media, and having Nigerian men tell me I look pretty and then ask me to accept wire transfers of large sums of money.

One could also correctly assume that I never quite expected to be writing a book about being fat, either.

Nobody really spends their childhood thinking about how awesome it would be to chronicle a lifetime of people watching you not fitting into things, asking if you are really going to eat that, and giving you tips on how not to be a hideous boil on the ass of society.

If anything, I figured I'd follow in the footsteps of Jane Austen, or at the very least come up with a "literary masterpiece" based on a peyote-induced dream I had once about angry teenage girls who fall in love with broody vampires.

But here we are. I am the writer I always wanted to be. And the subject is me and my life as a fat girl.

Overall, I'd like this book to help readers realize that being chubby your whole entire life doesn't mean you'll end up alone, unhappy, or the subject of some TLC medical show. And if you happen to be turned on by sociology, obesity isn't without its interesting aspects. For instance, being a fat kid afforded me the unique experience of witnessing the evolution of pejorative name-calling.

In elementary school, I was often called *cow, chubs,* or *tubby.* The latter two are adorable societal stigmas that might also double as the name of your pet hamster or determined cartoon tugboat.

High school labeled me as fat-ass or fat whore. Honestly, I think teen boys just like to mix together all the vulgar insults they know because they're insecure about things like ball hair or their legitimacy as white rappers. Classic projection.

In college, I was what was often considered a buffer or cockblocker, which is the technical term for the large physical barrier I often provided between my super-cute friends and the sleazy douchebags at the bar. It was primarily hurled around 3 A.M. as I escorted my barefoot roommates back to our dorm.

And then finally, I reached adulthood. The period of maturity when I assumed most forms of teasing and bullying had been outgrown, until I discovered the comments section of absolutely any news site or social network. *"What's that chubby adult woman? You feel pretty today? Really, that's weird because you look like Type 2 diabetes and rising healthcare costs."* Which is just a fancy adult way of saying I'm fat.

I feel like every fat-girl book on the shelf talks about how horrible being chubby is, then somewhere along the line, the author breaks up with gluten, buries her demons, and becomes one with the happy skinny girl who'd been inside her all along. I've actually long suspected there was a skinny girl inside me, but not in a metaphysical way. More like I probably had a twin, but I ate her.

This is not a diet book, guys. In fact, if I do this right, our cycles will align and we'll be eating our feelings together by the third chapter.

Instead, this book is full of hilarious and painfully true stories about my life as an overweight girl with an unconventional career path. I feel odd prematurely qualifying my own stories as hilarious, because you're an adult and you can make your own decisions, but my therapist says it's totally healthy, and I read, like, four chapters of this out loud to him and his eyes didn't glaze over once.

I think it's important to talk about things that make people feel awkward and uncomfortable, because that's how I navigate a good portion of my life, and misery loves company. Unless you're only coming over to talk about Jesus or sell me magazines from your kid's school, in which case, I'm good.

I'm going to talk about what it's like being the only chubby girl in a rural town in Ohio. I mean, there was this one other kid, but he had a legitimate thyroid issue, allegedly. And I am also going to talk about how I struggled with dating and relationships (fat girls suck at this as much as the skinny girls do, and we have more back fat), gave the middle finger to dieting, embraced an adorable case of anxiety disorder that led to me dropping out of college and trying to teach a pug to flush the toilet, learned about womanhood by failing at lesbianism, accidentally had three kids, figured out the secret to loving my curves, and became a nationally recognized body advocate.

Oh, and I'm also going to write a lot about sex and what my body looks like naked, and by the end, I'll show it to you. Hopefully you'll be entertained, and maybe inspired to get naked, too.

You just looked at the end of the book, didn't you? Reading the last page first is like not forwarding a chain letter. You just killed four people in Arkansas and none of your wishes will ever come true. Unless your wish was to see me naked, pervert.

1

I WAS BORN A POOR FAT CHILD

FIRST THINGS FIRST, I'm going to tell you why I'm fat, because I actually get this question a lot, much in the way people are asked how they got into live-action role playing or funeral home cosmetology. The answer I'd like to give to people who ask me that question is that God made us all different, and she made some people round-shaped, like me, and some people asshole-shaped, like you. Too direct? Fine, here's the deal.

Most kids inherit their best qualities from their parents. I inherited mental illness and fat thighs. Oh, and astigmatism and coarse body hair.

I have a friend whose brother makes millions harvesting deer semen from giant bucks that he then sells to other rich people so they can grow their own giant deer to then shoot and hang their heads on the wall. It's all very *Island of Dr. Moreau*. The point is, if my parents were deer, nobody would jerk them off. I mean, they're lovely people, but in terms of genetic sperm value, you might as well just put them out of their misery. Nobody likes chubby deer hooked on extended-release Xanax.

My father had been a state-ranked wrestler in high school. He still has the trophies on the dresser in his bedroom, and cauliflower ear on each side. A remnant left behind from the days of having his head smashed into mats and the sweaty body parts of other boys in spandex singlets. Despite being called what the authorities referred to back then as a longhair, a hippie pot head identified by his shaggy long locks, my dad was also built like an athlete. He stood six feet tall with thick muscular thighs and calves. It was the type of body that could go a decade or so with little upkeep and still be seen as in shape, then kinda in shape, and then just plain dense and heavy.

My mom was short like her Irish mother, but with the dark features of her Spanish father. She had all the making of a slender woman, long fingers and small hips, but due to severe bouts of depression spent most of her youth and adulthood at varying degrees of obesity. When she was stressed or upset, we ate more. When she was happy and upbeat, we ate more expensive food. I walked away from this combination with the pale porcelain skin of an Irish woman, a mental state that self-medicated with food, and the thighs of Hulk Hogan. I was fat because it was really easy for me to be fat.

Being an overweight child in the 1980s is nothing like it is now. We weren't tagged like animals and targeted on billboards or news stories about GMOs and high-fructose corn syrup. We flew under the radar with no real concern about athleticism or portion size. Sure, we weren't exactly desirable for things like dodgeball teams in gym class or the sexy covers of car magazines, but we weren't hurting anyone. Fat was a normal body shape for me, and after seeing my parents in their underwear, I knew thin was just not going to be in the cards.

I have been skinny only three times in my life.

1 At four months gestation.
2 After getting my stomach pumped as a toddler following the accidental ingestion of an industrial carpet cleaner my dad absent mindedly stored in a baby bottle.
3 Following a marginally successful run as a bulimic.

I remember there was a period of time when I assumed I was, like everyone else, normal looking. You don't exactly go into kindergarten expecting to build an entourage of attractive rich friends. You glob together with a shared interest in the alphabet, sandboxes, and head lice. And so life went on like that, friendships formed based on logistics and the year in which we all collectively fell from our mother's vaginas. We were friends not because of how pretty we were, but because of 1981.

All of that changed when my parents decided to become small business owners, or a period of time I like to call "When We Became Poor." Prior to this moment, we bounced in and out of the lower middle class regularly. My father worked in maintenance for the Ohio Turnpike, my mother did the bookkeeping for my grandmother's bridal salon, and we lived in a three-bedroom ranch on three wooded acres gifted to us by my grandparents. Incapable of saving money, my dad drove a leased BMW and my mom ordered preppy duck boots from fancy magazines even though we often didn't have enough for groceries or utility bills. After receiving a windfall settlement from the airport after the flight path of a cargo company began flying so low that the plane vibrations cracked the walls and windows of our house and filled our bedrooms with the stench of jet fuel, my parents decided to forgo typical investment opportunities and instead put the money into what my father repeatedly assured us was the "flourishing entertainment sector." When he would say that around the dinner table or at family gatherings, his eyes would light up and he'd reflexively rub his hands together like Scrooge McDuck counting gold coins. I feel the need to add a disclaimer here to mention that my parents are really amazing people; they just make terrible financial decisions.

Video Exchange was housed in a tiny strip mall between a dingy bar and a cowboy supply store. In an Ohio town of three thousand people, this was the third video rental store to open. There were officially more video stores than gas stations. Video Exchange felt millions of miles away from the flourishing entertainment sector my dad promised. It was a depressing establishment, dark wood-paneled walls, cheap black shelves lined with empty laminated movie boxes, and a rusty carnival-themed popcorn machine on the counter.

The back room housed the actual videotapes on bookcases jammed with rows and rows of numbered plastic cases. Even though I was seven and had absolutely no involvement in the purchase of an eight-hundred-square-foot VHS rental store, every day after school and on weekends the back room became my life. This is actually a pretty normal situation when your family owns a business, sinks all your savings into it, and therefore can't afford to hire employees. Providing child labor can sometimes mean the difference between having electricity in your house or not.

Unfortunately for my parents, the new business owner euphoria had a shelf life of about six months, and then it became painfully clear why my dad had gotten such a great deal on a roomful of video tapes: nobody wanted them. Despite numerous renovations, new paint, and flashy Hollywood movie signs, the business continued to struggle, and my little brother and I became unintended victims of its downward spiral. Money became so tight we traded in our BMW for a used station wagon. We stopped opening our pool each summer because the upkeep was too expensive. The depression and stress in our home were palpable. I remember my friend Laura and I walking in after school one day to find my dad crying in the kitchen. Seeing your parents cry is a very uncomfortable experience that makes you also, reflexively, cry. It's Pavlovian.

Within a year, our lives had changed completely. I wasn't seeing my friends as much; between maintaining their full-time jobs and the business, my parents no longer had time to take us to soccer practice; and dinner became my brother and I schlepping half a mile down a busy highway to McDonald's and eating in the back room of the video store while watching sports-themed kids movies. *Rookie of the Year, Angels in the Outfield, Little Giants, The Big Green, Ladybugs, The Mighty Ducks* . . . the nineties was a decade made for preteen athletic underdogs with little to no parental supervision.

Now, before you get all riled up, I'm not blaming McDonald's for my obesity; it's just that when you are a kid who is suddenly inactive and living close to the poverty line in the back of a video store, fresh veggies are expensive and chicken nuggets take a toll. You would think my parents would have been concerned about my growing waistline, but they said nothing. Although I come from a household that struggled with weight, I didn't grow up on diets. My mom was never overly feminine, opting instead for short hair and sensible jeans and sweatshirts, so vanity and fad diets were never really her thing. I remember asking her once if she would join the local Jazzercise studio like my friend Audrey's mom, because Audrey said that while the parents worked out, the kids got to hang out in the playroom and play free arcade games. My mom brushed it off as too expensive and said if she wanted to work out, she had a perfectly good Jane Fonda vinyl record at home she could stretch to. This was true, my mother did own that record, but she never stretched out to it. Instead I'd pull it off the shelf and stare at skinny, feather-haired Jane and wonder where she hid her pubic hair in all those high-waisted leotards. The point is, if my parents didn't recognize I was overweight, how was I supposed to?

ZHIRA IS RUSSIAN FOR FAT

The summer I was eight, my parents took my brother and me on vacation to an antiquated mobile home park in Myrtle Beach, South Carolina, in a borrowed RV. The majority of the inhabitants of this park were retirees who spent their days driving around in golf carts and walking the early morning beach with metal detectors. I was able to befriend two girls around my age, Mischa and Marlena, who were there visiting their Russian grandmother in the campsite behind ours.

Mischa was younger than me, with thin tanned arms and a short blond bowl cut. Marlena was slightly older, with dark curly hair that fell to her shoulders and summer freckles across her cheeks. I loved going over to their camper at night. Their grandma would braid my hair while we ate powdery spiced cookies and she talked about all the men she slept with during the war. I don't even know what war she was talking about. I just assumed there always was one back then. If there wasn't, old people would basically have nothing to talk about besides "Oh hey, I got polio again."

After dinner the three of us would walk the paved loop around the beachside community, talking about makeup and our favorite New Kid on the Block, mine of course being Danny, an early foreshadowing of my preference for men with mouths built for cunnilingus. One night two boys on bikes stopped in front of us and asked our names. Talking to boys was only mildly exciting to me at this point, even though I only had four of them in my class, and they were about as appealing as my brother. We chatted about the ocean and the warm weather, and then one of the boys asked Marlena if she had a boyfriend, and after she answered no, I added that I didn't have one, either.

Then he looked at me and said, "Well yeah, because you're fat."

In that moment, every part of my body felt different. I became acutely aware that the shorts I was wearing had ridden up between my thighs and that the waistband was leaving indentations on my hips. That the fat that had started to accumulate in my breasts wasn't perky, but rather made them sag horizontally across my chest into my armpits. My tummy was not just pale and soft, but bulbous and unattractive.

Suddenly, something had been put out into the universe, and there was no takes-backsies. Like that quote by Alice Hoffman, "Once you know some things, you can't unknow them."

That's totally what happened when I found out that ducks pee, poop, and have sex all in one hole. They are also massive rapists. It was a traumatizing realization, and I can never like ducks again. It's also exactly what being told I was fat felt like. My days went from thinking about normal kid stuff to obsessing over my body and what people were saying about it.

Was I the one blamed for passing gas during silent reading time in school because fat people are grosser and fart more than skinny people?

Did the boys in gym fight to not be my square-dancing partner, you know, the equivalent of child marriage, because I was chunkier than the other girls?

Anxiety over my looks consumed me, and suddenly being fat went from a private issue I struggled with to a medical one as I stood on the scale in gym class during the annual fitness test and was officially crowned the first kid in third grade to reach 100 pounds. A century ago, my weight would have meant I was wealthy and fertile, with access to actual doctors and nondiseased meats. Now it meant there was something wrong with me, as the kids behind me audibly gasped while my gym teacher fumbled with the metal slider on the scale before squinting at the numbers a final time and recording them onto his clipboard. I thought that his record keeping meant the whole embarrassing experience was over with, but by the end of the day a sealed envelope was sent home in my folder explaining the perils of childhood obesity to my parents with a list of helpful tips to aid in my fun journey to a new, healthy lifestyle.

1. Incorporate wheat bread into your child's lunches.
2. Park farther away from malls and restaurants to encourage walking and fitness.
3. Have your child complete their nightly homework standing up.
4. Replace all your forks with chopsticks.
5. Write the word "NO!" on a piece of paper and tape it to the front of the fridge as a gentle reminder that they are not allowed to snack.
6. Have your child eat slowly in front of a full-length mirror to mimic the public shame they'd feel while being fat in cafeteria situations.

These are tips that I still get to this very day, only instead of sealed envelopes from my gym teacher, they come from strangers on the Internet. Why was I fat? I was fat because being fat was what we could afford to be, and being fat was easier than facing whatever stress was happening at home.

So now that you know the *why*, how about the *why still*. Why am I still overweight? Well, in the simplest of terms, I like to eat food, and I'm really good at it, so as a result, I eat like a girl who thinks she has the metabolism of a Kenyan marathoner. Also, the thing about dieting is that it's really horrible and boring for a longer period of time than feeling pretty in small jeans feels. That's just basic math.

2

HONESTLY, I DIDN'T HAVE A CHANCE

WHEN YOU GET into your twenties and begin to take a mental stock of your life, the good parts and the bad parts become glaringly apparent. We all have them, good parts and bad parts, but your twenties are generally the first time that you really begin to see the timeline that led you to your current existence. It's what all obnoxious, first-time voting, finally out on our own, we know how the world works, pseudo-adults do. We gather up our parents' flaws and lay them across the table like a poker hand in the ultimate game of WHO'S MORE FUCKED-UP.

It is this very moment that led many of my friends to freak out and seek a steady therapist by twenty-three. Having already been over a decade deep into therapy myself, I was past the notion that I'd ever be "fixed," and was instead aiming for the much more achievable goal of "pleasant to be around in normal society." It sounds easy, but if you knew my family, you'd realize that it was not. Sure, everyone says they grow up in crazy families, but I am happy to provide medical data and empty prescription bottles to back up my claims.

I grew up in Swanton, Ohio, a small town about thirty minutes outside Toledo. It's a rural area characterized by cornfields, the empty buildings that once housed small manufacturing businesses, and the words "I'm leaving and never coming back" wistfully inscribed by angsty seniors in the backs of yearbooks over many decades. But Swanton is not without its charm. There is a quiet beauty in the vintage buildings that line Main Street, and a certain sense of safety that comes with knowing everyone, as well as probably being related to them.

The only thing stopping me from saying that I've lived here my whole life is the fact that when I was an infant, my parents allegedly moved to Palm Springs, California, for my dad's job, and one time in a supermarket, Jackie Coogan, the guy who played Uncle Fester on *The Addams Family*, asked my mom if he could hold me and told me I was pretty. We moved back to Swanton shortly after that, and while I have no actual memory of the experience, it was that temporary glimmer of hope and a faded Polaroid of me and my dad in front of a palm tree that fed my inherent belief that I did not belong here. It also had me doing really douchey things like demanding to cover California for our fourth-grade geography project, you know, because I was "from there."

Unlike Palm Springs, Swanton was a relatively conservative town and could easily have served as the inspiration for the movie *Footloose*. My household was a mixed bag, my mom being Irish Catholic and my dad a liberal agoraphobic. My parents were high school sweethearts, and when I was growing up my mom would tell me stories about falling in love with my father, who was poor and from a large family, shortly after she had moved to Swanton with her wealthy parents.

"When I met him," she'd say, laughing wistfully, "he had no shoes. I had to buy him shoes."

The stories were always funny and adorable, and a stark contrast to the actual den of religious guilt, sexual tension, and mental illness I was being raised in. Half the time, I think she was telling the stories, not for my benefit, but to remind herself why she was still in this mess to begin with.

In 1983 my dad was hit by a semi-truck. You weren't expecting that, were you? Don't worry, he's alive. I haven't spoken to him yet today, but he was alive yesterday when I was over there showing him how to use his DVR. So, as of yesterday, he was alive.

I was two, and my mother was nine months pregnant with my brother. My dad worked for the maintenance department of the Ohio Turnpike, and one day a semi driver fell asleep and veered into a work crew, killing the man in front of my dad, and then slamming into my father, throwing him twenty-five feet headfirst into a giant compressor. He had been running a jackhammer. The flagman never warned him and he never heard it coming.

My dad was left in a coma, his left lung was crushed, he suffered a massive brain injury, and his shoulder and left side were destroyed. I was sent to live with my mom's cousin on a farm in western Ohio while my mother gave birth alone to a baby she refused to name until my dad was able to meet him.

When my father finally woke up, it was a month before he consistently remembered who my mother was, and when he was taken to see my brother, he declared he wanted to name the baby Sherman T. Potter, the old guy from *M*A*S*H,* not the one that dressed up like a lady, although that would have made for a much funnier story. Eventually, my mom talked him into the name Adam, and after two months in the hospital and six more in various rehabilitation facilities, my father came home.

I don't know if you've ever lived with someone who suffered a traumatic brain injury before, but it's like winning a Publishers Clearing House drawing, only instead of a big check, they show up on your doorstep with Gary Busey and then run away before you can give him back. If you were to ask my mom what happened the day of the accident, she'd tell you my father died. As in, that one guy who lived in our house and had sex with my mom before the semi-truck hit him.

My dad was able to return to work in a limited capacity, leaving the labor-intensive maintenance department to work in tolls, but he was often in and out of reconstructive surgeries and residential rehab trying to regain use of his shoulder and arm and life. It was all very superficial. Nothing could repair what had been done to him psychologically or mentally. In rare moments, I caught glimpses of the man my mom referred to as "old dad." The engaging guy who swung us around by our arms, collapsing into dizzy piles of giggles and reading us *Grimm's Fairy Tales* until we fell asleep under forts made of bedsheets. Most of the time, I got "new dad," the transient man would go on manic benders of rash decisions and financial free fall before spending entire weeks anxious and locked in his bedroom watching old episodes of *Saturday Night Live,* forgetting to pick me up from school or what year it was.

This is not to say his short-term memory loss didn't work to my advantage a time or two. Like in junior high when I had a parent conference after slapping a girl in the face for calling me a fat Tori

Spelling. My dad never showed up, and after sitting in the office waiting for thirty minutes, the assistant principal, who looked like a balding Geraldo Rivera, assumed my outburst was due to absent parenting and let me leave out of pity. But on the same token, it was devastating when my dad would forget birthdays or miss soccer games because he was too paranoid to leave the house.

My dad was often between medications, leaving his moods unpredictable and running full throttle. The majority of my childhood can be described as walking into a room having no idea who was going to be in there waiting for me. Our home life had become dictated by his cycle of manic highs and lows. We'd hit a period of time when he was kind and excited about life. He'd buy fancy cars, and businesses, and take us on fun vacations. There were the little moments you just expect to happen within families that stand out as limited but treasured stones I could hold on the palm of my hand. Kissing my mom before she left for work. Seeing a picture of me from college and telling me I had a pretty smile. Taking my brother and me to see Bill Cosby perform live at a local theater. These were normal dad things.

Then we'd hit a pothole and he'd just shut off. His demeanor became mean and he'd levy cutting jabs about our appearance, and how difficult we'd all made his life on a daily basis. He'd accuse my mother of cheating on him if she'd forget to call to check in, and then he'd announce to my brother and me that she'd left us and was never coming back. He'd get frustrated with everyday tasks and communicate that by throwing the phone or remote at the wall. He'd stop leaving the house or helping with its upkeep, hoarding frivolous paperwork and documents in brown boxes he'd stack in his bedroom and office. Money would grow tight because of his inability to handle finances and work consistently, so broken items would stay broke, like remotes held together with duct tape or holes in the walls and torn window screens. I'd come home from school to find our electricity or gas turned off, and our phone shrill and shrieking as bill collectors called at all hours of the day. I lay in bed anxious for 9 P.M. to come each evening, since that's the hour when the calls would finally stop.

As much as I love my dad, growing up in that house was exhausting and overcrowded. The mental illness and cycling emotions were far too heavy for me. My mom, who carried the stress of dealing with my father and two children, had already lost her sister to depression and suicide, and was becoming increasingly depressed herself. She often explained away his outbursts with "He's just scared and confused," "He doesn't realize what he's saying," or "Sometimes it's like he's a big child." Many nights I'd hear her crying through the thin wall between our bedrooms after a volatile fight over finances or my dad's behavior. It was harder for her to separate the two versions of my dad in her head, and I'd get mad at her inability to stand up to him. Only as an adult can I appreciate how difficult it must be to have to see every single day the face of the man you are essentially mourning.

When something traumatic happens, like your dad getting hit by a semi-truck, there is a grace period where people treat you with kid gloves and understanding nods. For me, that was about three years, which is three seconds in brain injury time. By then, everyone assumes things are all patched up and back to normal, which meant I was no longer that little girl eating her emotions from that poor family who had that horrible accident, but rather, that chubby emo girl with the weird dad who sometimes never leaves the house and screams at people in banks. Brain injuries are for life, like those gangs in prison you get raped into. The bad parts are always there, like tattoos, the good parts buried deep inside, lining the insides of my ribs so I can breathe every day.

It's those sweet and sour moments that make up life with my father.

KEITH BUCKENMEYER, KITTEN KILLER

In fourth grade I became obsessed with Lewis Carroll's *Alice's Adventures in Wonderland*, as I was very much feeling like a bored girl hungry for adventure myself. As my birthday approached, I made it clear that this was the year I wanted a cat like Alice.

My mom always bred cocker spaniels and pugs, and you couldn't throw a rock in my house and not hit a whelping dog. (*Whelping*, by the way, is a fancy dog term for giving birth, which is a scenario that happened during much of my adolescence on the linoleum of our kitchen floor. I still can't eat my mom's spaghetti.) We were decidedly dog-people, and my mother reminded me of this every time I answered what I wanted for my birthday.

"Just a cat, please."

"You're not getting a cat, dammit," she'd reply exasperated. "And besides, I'm allergic to their dander. Having a cat in the house would kill me."

On April 28, 1991, I rolled over at around 6 A.M. to find my dad quietly sitting beside my bed, which was jarring. Anytime you wake up and find a six-foot-tall man with a blond mustache staring at you while you sleep is jarring.

"Happy birthday," he whispered. "I was thinking you and I could go and pick out a special present today, just us; a secret present."

I just realized how creepy that looks written out. Kids, if a man with facial hair sneaks into your room and asks you to go with him to get a "secret present," don't go. Unless that strange man is your dad and he's taking you to the humane society to get a cat because your mom is mean, in which case, yes, definitely go.

The seat belt was the only physical restraint holding me in my seat on the way to shelter as I bounced in excitement, singing Jim Croce's "Bad, Bad Leroy Brown" with reckless abandon, shouting the cuss words extra loud because I knew my dad wouldn't say anything. It was a surreal experience, not only being alone with my dad doing something special, but also going to the humane society. We lived in the country and the "Free Kittens" signs were only outnumbered by the "Free Bunnies Dead or Alive" signs, which I never quite understood until high school when I got a tattoo from a guy who had an albino boa constrictor that devoured a rabbit in the tank next to me as I lay on his kitchen table getting a blurry butterfly etched into my hip. It was an agonizingly slow process, on both accounts.

Walking into the shelter was a shock. I had really built it up in my head as some sort of happy cat utopia, but everything smelled like stale pee and the sawdust janitors put down when someone pukes in school. All the cats looked old and scraggly, like feline versions of my drunk uncle Jay, whom we don't invite to Christmas anymore because he once rummaged through our drawers for change, threw up in my closet, and half passed out while touching himself in our shower. I couldn't appreciate at that age how truly badass this guy was, and now he's sober, has found Jesus, and works as a magician and balloon animal maker at nursing homes. I knew you when, Uncle Jay.

I stood at the entrance frozen in anxiety until my dad put his arm around my shoulder and pulled me in tight, and I was suddenly calm because he always smells like sweat and freshly sanded wood. He walked slowly up and down the aisles of rusty metal cages, stopping every so often to stick his finger through the bars and play with the eager cat batting at him for attention. I finally decided on a small kitten with fluffy orange fur, minimal eye goop, and a smoker's cough.

Overwhelmed with guilt and homeless cat empathy, my father sent me to wait the car while he paid, appearing at the passenger door a short time later with a small cardboard box riddled with air holes and the word *Sunshine* scribbled across the front with a Sharpie. What a ridiculous name for a cat. On the car ride home, I used the pen from the glove compartment to cross out Sunshine and rename her Kimberly, which is what I was legally changing my name to the second I turned eighteen. Kimberly and I bonded the whole trip home as I whispered to her through the tiny holes in her container.

We returned home to find my mom and brother waiting on the porch. This is what we did before the Internet, by the way. Sometimes we just sat outside and looked at nothing for hours at a time. My mom was visibly unhappy when she saw the box, but what could you do, I had legally adopted Kimberly; it was official, she was mine. I excitedly ran to the front porch to show my brother the box and let him peer through the holes while my dad went to the garage to get a box and a blanket, a peace offering to my mother to keep the cat outside. It wasn't an ideal situation, but it was a cat, so I would make do.

Then it all went pear-shaped. When my dad removed the lid of

Kimberly's box, she lunged at him, clawing him across the cheek and darting off across the grass, scaling the thirty-foot oak tree in our yard. My dad was furious, vomiting curse words and wiping blood from his face with a rag. I was hysterical, screaming her name and chasing after her to the base of the tree, pleading with her to come down and shaking her food bowl. My mom took my dad inside to clean up his wounds, but I refused to leave the tree, staring up at the orange ball of fur wedged on one of the highest branches. An hour later, my dad came back outside.

"Listen, I don't think she's coming down right now," he said. "Maybe if we leave her alone for a while, she won't be scared and she'll climb back down on her own."

"Don't you have a ladder you could use?" I asked.

"No," he replied, running his hands along the wounds on his neck and cheek. "That is much taller than any ladder I have. You'd need a cherry-picker to reach that high."

"Can't you get one of those?"

"No, those are really expensive."

I refused to budge, and defeated, he went back into the house, peeking out the window every so often to find me lying on the ground, croaking "Kimberllyyyy" with what was left of my voice, my hysterical sobs now just dry, snotty hiccups.

Two hours later, he rejoined me at the bottom of the tree.

"I called a buddy with a cherry-picker we can rent; he'll be here in a bit."

I hugged my dad for what was probably the third time in my life, and asked him to keep an eye on the cat while I ran inside for water because sacrificing your body for a cause was totally dehydrating.

When the cherry-picker arrived, I watched my dad being slowly lifted into the air, as I stood at the bottom of the tree, holding the kitten's unworn pink collar. When he reached the top, I expected a heartfelt reunion, but instead, as he reached to pull Kimberly from the branch, she screamed like a human, bit his hand, and then fell to the ground. It was the most horrific animal experience my eyes had ever seen, save for *Howard the Duck,* which was terrifying even before I grasped the basic concept of bestiality.

Kimberly was an orange lump of fur, flipping around on the ground, unable to stand or use her legs. By the time my dad had reached the ground, he told my mom to take me inside and to get his shovel. I insisted I be allowed to tell her good-bye, and my brother followed me over to gawk at her as she hissed.

"Good-bye, Kimberly; these six hours we had together were the best and most disturbing hours of my life. I love you so much. Please say hi to great-grandma for me when you get to heaven; her name is Margaret and she has a lazy eye. But, if you go to separate animal heaven, then totally don't worry about it," I tearfully whispered beside her.

"Hey, look, she has balls; she's not even a girl!" my brother exclaimed.

"Shut up, Adam," my dad warned as my mother ushered us into the house so he could finish the deed, burying her in a shallow grave in the field behind our house. The next morning, just at dawn, he woke me up to collect flowers from our garden and showed me her tiny grave. He stood there while I cried into his jacket. It was one of his kindest and most human moments, and it happened after he murdered my transsexual cat with a shovel.

NO OFFENSE, BUT YOUR DAD'S A PSYCHO

Our high school employed what is known as block scheduling. It split our year into halves, meaning we took fewer classes for longer periods of time. For example, we had a set of only three classes each day, but then those classes would end midway through the year, and we'd get a new set of three. We had fewer subjects to juggle, which was great. On the flip side, if you hated a class, you were stuck in it for hours.

I walked into my second week of Anatomy & Physiology much like I always did, head down with my thighs rubbing together, but also with a tummy full of butterflies. Anat & Phys was my favorite class, not because of science—in fact, I was horrible and pretty sure I was failing—but because of a senior named Steve, whom I'd had a crush on. He was a giant redheaded football player who sat beside me in class, making me feel small in comparison. A feat I relished. We spent most of the three hour class chatting about the tests and computer assignments the teacher, Mrs. Pierson, a chill long-haired bohemian woman who took a very laissez-faire approach to teaching, would toss our way to complete as we saw fit. Again, this might explain why I failed science, but I should add here that Steve went on to play NFL football and now works for NASCAR, which only serves to make this entire ordeal that much more embarrassing.

I walked into class one day and set my books down at our table of four.

"Yeah, you can't sit with us anymore," Steve announced.

"Why?" I asked, panicking.

"Gosh, I don't know, because your psycho dad just tried to fight me in the parking lot?"

He coninuted to speak as the blood in my body rushed to my feet. I felt heavy and lumbering as I slowly nodded my head and backed away to Mrs. Pierson's desk.

"My stomach hurts," I explained as she nodded and thoughtlessly handed me a hall pass to the office.

I called my mother and frantically explained I was ill, and waited in the office to be picked up as I replayed the events Steve had spat at me in my head. He and my father had both arrived at a four-way stop intersection, and my dad felt Steve didn't stop enough. So he followed Steve in his station wagon, screaming at him to pull over, which was actually a normal form of communication for my dad, who was fluent in road rage. When Steve parked in the student parking lot, my dad burst out of his car, screaming at him to learn to drive and challenging him to fight. The details are also a bit murky on whether or not he had actual pants on; again, not wearing pants is a normal thing for my dad. He only went through drive-throughs, so pants and shoes were generally unnecessary.

I was hysterical the entire ride home, screaming the story to my mother, who interjected calmly that it probably wasn't as dramatic as I was making it sound and that everyone would probably forget about it by tomorrow. She obviously didn't remember how high school worked.

I burst through the front door to find my dad asleep facedown in bed. I furiously climbed on top of him, pulling his hair, sobbing into his back, begging him to please just wake up and be a normal dad and stop ruining my life. He woke up and looked at me, my thick black eyeliner running down my face and dripping off my chin onto his white T-shirt. It was as if he were a lost sandy-haired four-year-old with a mustache. He looked confused and wounded and I immediately felt guilty. My mom was right; in that moment he didn't know better.

It's not that he didn't care that high school was already horrible for me and he was making it worse; it's that he had no idea he was doing it in the first place.

People like me grow up promising to leave their hometowns and never come back, and also hide the fact that we flinch at the first hint of public humiliation. The thickness of our therapy file makes us members of an elite club of millions from adorably dysfunctional families. You can spot us by the special notes written and pinned to our shirts.

"If lost, return to Ohio. Don't mind the guy who answers the door to claim me, he's not supposed to have pants on, anyway."

3

FINDING YOUR TRIBE AND OTHER ASSHOLEY FEEL-GOOD EXPRESSIONS YOUR PARENTS PUSH ON YOU

IT WAS MY twelfth birthday, and I was standing on a chair wearing a bedazzled sombrero as a crowd of waiters circled me, singing in unison. My mom looked up from her seat laughing and mouthing the words, "Isn't this fun?"

Honestly, it had never been fun. Any situation that included putting a disco ball on the heads of children and having them stand on chairs and be cheered at like small fat piñatas was panic attack inducing. I looked around the restaurant at the faces of people drawn over by the spectacle. At some tables parents with small kids and elderly couples clapped along. A couple on a date in the corner looked annoyed by the noise. And a six top of girls just a bit younger than me watched giggling and pointing, not in disgust, but in anticipation. Later that evening, the birthday brigade would make its way to their table, singing their chant to a group of happy and ecstatic friends, excited to be there together and celebrating.

I was there with my mom, my brother, and my best friend, Laura

Burress. Laura and I had met in kindergarten, and every year since she remained my closest friend. Laura was the only girl from my grade whom I'd let come over to my house, because she wasn't weirded out by my dad, she didn't care that sometimes we had to walk next door to pee because our water had been shut off, and she still liked to play Barbies, even though most of the girls in our grade had started to grow out of them.

"Happy happy happy birthday. Happy happy happy birthday. Happy happy happy birthday to you. To you. To you. Ole!" The staff cheered before immediately dispersing back to their previous tasks.

"Look here," Our server waved, and as my eyes met hers she aimed her camera up at me and snapped a Polaroid from the ground. Shaking it with one hand, she helped me down, tossed the photo on the table, and took the sombrero from my head. It has to be the single worst photo ever taken of me in my life.

Chi-Chi's was the Olive Garden of Mexican restaurants. The buildings were covered in brightly colored stucco and stuffed full of overzealous stereotypes and tacky décor. It was like eating inside a pair of Skidz pants. Although the chain would later close in the United States due to a massive outbreak of food poisoning and hepatitis A, Chi-Chi's was a staple for almost all of my childhood birthdays. I'd also go on to have my very first legal alcoholic beverage there, a frozen peach margarita with a sword of maraschino cherries and a large pink umbrella. A drink so girly, I started menstruating after two sips.

When we returned home that evening, my mom sat on the couch with a photo album and carefully taped the Polaroid to the page. One, two, three, four, five, six. Six Chi-Chi's birthday Polaroids. Photographic evidence that at least once a year, my childhood was exciting. The reality was it's hard to have birthday parties at your house when it's full of barking dogs and it's a lot easier to pretend you have a lot of friends when you're in a busy Mexican restaurant surrounded by people paid to clap for you.

"Mom, I don't want to go to Chi-Chi's for my birthday anymore," I announced. Laura, who came from a quiet family that rarely exhibited any form of confrontation or speaking above library level, shifted uncomfortably on the love seat next to me.

"What are you talking about?! You love having your birthday at Chi-Chi's." She looked genuinely hurt and surprised.

"No, I like baskets of salty chips and fried ice cream. I don't like standing on chairs and being sung to like a baby. It's stupid; you're making me look stupid and either you don't realize it or you don't care," I spat. It came out meaner than I had intended, but the fact is that twelve was a really hard birthday for me. It was my first year in a new school without any friends. Prior to seventh grade, due to what I can only assume was a desperate act of penance on the part of my mother, my brother and I spent our elementary years in Catholic school. This was an unexpected move, as we were the types of Catholics who rarely went to church outside of school mass, but when we did, my dad would have to go out and buy a new suit and my mom would cry in the pew the whole time as she recited the rosary. I would have been embarrassed had it not been for Mara Riley's family, who came to church so seldom, her dad wore his wedding tuxedo and black tennis shoes to Mass on Christmas.

Catholic school really suited me. Not because I was deeply religious or passionate about the faith; when my classmates would put their heads down in prayer for the sick and the dying, I'd clench my eyes shut and pray that my hair would go straight and my boobs would shrink. But a certain part of me was excited at the thought of having every facet of my life become a potentially terrifying experience, because almost everything in the Catholic faith was a terrifying experience. Spontaneous pregnancy, murder, people's heads falling off, some guy circumcised himself, it was bananas.

Catholic school was a safe place for me. The classes were small and we all wore uniforms. That really leveled the societal playing field because, let's face it, nobody looks any better than anyone else in pleated khaki pants, and in general, it's easier to deal with body insecurities in a class of eight, three of which you are related to.

Unfortunately, twelve years of Catholic school tuition was not in our budget, so once I hit junior high, I was pulled from the safety and comfort of my cushy private elementary school and placed in the local public school. I went from a class of eight to a class of 120. The uniforms that had so easily disguised my body insecurities and discomfort were now stripped away, leaving me suddenly responsible for expressing my personal style through fashionable clothing and trendy hairstyles. That is easier to do if the only other female influence in your house doesn't dry her hair with those men's hair dryers with the brush already attached.

Laura was still attending the private Catholic school my parents could no longer afford, and seeing her on the weekends and birthdays wasn't enough to stop me from being lonely and homesick for my old life.

Swanton Junior High was a large three-story building attached to the high school in the center of town. It was the first newly renovated school building in Swanton, though, like Chi-Chi's, it would later be closed down and condemned, in this case due to exposed wires and asbestos. Apropos, I'm probably dying of asbestosis right now.

While a few of my Catholic school classmates made the jump to public school with me, they had somehow landed into piles of existing friends, and aside from their smiling at me in the lunch line or making an inside joke about elementary school while awkwardly stuck as my partner in science lab, our past ties had been severed and forgotten. That hurt. When you grow up in a class of twelve people, and three or four of you are put into a completely new environment, you expect a sense of camaraderie. There was none. They showed up to seventh grade suddenly sexually mature and years ahead of me in mainstream fashion and emotional cutting. These were things we were supposed to figure out together in the backs of school buses and during all-girl sleepovers. My parents understood none of that.

Long after the evening's awkwardness had subsided and Laura had gone home, my mom came to my room for one of her many pep talks.

"It's only April and it's still new." She rubbed my leg as she sat down next to me on my bed. We weren't affectionate people, so even as she tried to be endearing, it came off as awkward and forced. "New takes time. You'll make friends; you just have to find your tribe."

"Finding your tribe" has recently made its return as a buzz phrase. It's used at social media conferences to refer to the group of people who find connectivity and solidarity among their online communities. Maybe they all knit or breastfeed in public or have open marriages.

When you are a kid, you don't really have any defining qualities outside of what your parents pass down, which basically meant I was fucked, as previously noted. Unless, perhaps, there were other preteens whose fathers handwrote hate mail to PepsiCo when they discontinued Crystal Pepsi?

I went into seventh grade slightly overweight, with large wire glasses, a gap between my front teeth, and an extraordinarily large collection of vests. Oh, and a perm. This was during the era when hairdressers still convinced you that curly hair was more controllable if you permed it. We should be rounding them up the same way we round up war criminals and Nazi sympathizers.

My mom called seventh grade a transition year, and told me to be more proactive. I called it hell, but was willing to give it a try.

I'VE GOT SPIRIT, HOW ABOUT YOU?

Right off the bat, there were four glaringly obvious differences between private and public school.

1 My chair in homeroom looked like somebody had had an abortion on it.
2 None of my teachers wanted to exchange phone numbers over spring break.
3 Ninety percent of my day was no longer spent highlighting stuff in Bibles.
4 We had pep rallies for everything.

In Catholic school, we never had pep rallies. We had crucifixion reenactments and Oxfam days where we pretended to live in third-world countries and ate bowls of rice on the floor, but no pep rallies. Our athletics were offered through CYO (Catholic Youth Organization) and consisted of same-sex teams globbed together from surrounding parishes. There wasn't a lot of skill or talent necessary; all were accepted and every game began with a blessing and ended in a convenient tie. In fourth grade, the girls were allowed to participate in a form of cheerleading. We showed up in our plaid uniform skirts and white T-shirts to shout excitedly along the sidelines at our struggling players. It was a less pornographic version of that Britney Spears video. We didn't do any jumps or choreographed dances, and the only formal indication of our existence was the inclusion of a black-and-white team photo in the back of our school yearbook. Nevertheless, it was official enough that we called ourselves cheerleaders.

That false sense of superiority is the only reason I can offer for voluntarily signing up for seventh-grade cheerleading tryouts. That or I suffered some kind of stroke that temporarily impaired my judgment. Seventh-grade cheerleading in a public school was not the same thing as CYO cheerleading. These girls were half gymnast, half Kardashian. I, on the other hand, had the flexibility and stamina of Jonah Hill.

As part of the requirements, you had to show up with your hair in a high ponytail, know how to do two signature kicks, and prepare a unique cheer to perform in front of the judges. I was pretty confident about that last part, because I was really good at rhyming, on account of my impeccable timing. Get it? This was going to be amazing. On the night of the tryout, my mom eased our van to a stop in front of the gym doors, looked me dead in the eyes, and said, "Hey, it's fine if you don't make it, okay?" I now realize that was her maternal way of saying, *There's no way this shit is happening.*

Our school mascot was the Fighting Bulldog, and our colors were purple and white, which I'd tried to incorporate in the white cotton shorts I'd stolen from my mom's cruise-wear drawer and my dad's long purple polo that hung off my shoulders and was loosely knotted at the bottom right side. Was I the only girl there wearing her parents' clothing? Yes I was.

When it was finally my turn, I gently patted the five thousand bobby pins holding the stubby ponytail atop my head, smiled brightly, and excitedly bounced onto the auditorium stage. Two adult coaches, Mrs. Dominique and Mrs. Rose, who both had daughters auditioning that night and had been themselves cheerleaders, made up the panel of judges. The current high school cheerleading captain also joined them, though she looked mostly irritated to be there. I introduced myself, did a high kick and a very loose interpretation of a Russian toe touch, and then began my cheer.

"Take your shot! It won't go in! You better get on your bus, again! Or we're gonna kick you in your D-O-G-S . . . what does that spell? SUCCESS!"

Panting and glistening with sweat, I clapped spiritedly as the three judges stared at me blankly.

"I'm sorry." Mrs. Rose finally broke the silence. "Did you say you were going to kick them in their dogs? Like their wieners?"

Prior to that moment, it hadn't occurred to me that I'd made up a cheer about wieners. I smiled brightly and did one final half-hearted toe touch before stepping out of the glaring spotlight and quietly returned to the holding area backstage. Some girls were practicing complicated jumps and cheers in front of a wall-length mirror. A small group who had witnessed my tryout stood laughing and whispering in the corner. I sat on a folding chair and began obsessively picking at an invisible spot on my white shorts, closing my eyes every so often to mentally whisper a prayer to God, asking him to please just let me make the squad. I had no pop culture reference for this at the time, but I can now confidently say that what I did onstage that evening was the equivalent of absolutely any humorous musical montage of dorky fat girls trying out for the squad of all seventeen *Bring It On* movies.

About an hour later, Mrs. Dominque clacked across the wood floors with her snakeskin heels, smiling and winking as she made her way to the chalkboard, pressing the white paper onto it with masking tape. The girls rushed the sign, squealing and yelling across the room to their friends. I slowly made my way to the chalkboard, running my finger down the list of girls. My name wasn't on the team roster, not even as an alternate, not even as the girl in charge of lining up the pom-poms on the sidelines when the real cheerleaders weren't using them.

"What's the matter, Brittany, someone kick you in your *wiener*?" one varsity girl laughed as she walked out surrounded by her fellow freshly minted cheerleaders.

I sat back down on the edge of my folding chair in the now-emptying choir room until Mrs. Rose came in to turn off the lights.

"Oh hun, is your mama not here yet?" she purred sympathetically.

"I'm not sure. I was actually wondering if you had picked anyone to be the school mascot yet?" I asked, pushing the thick wire glasses back up my still-sweaty face. "I was a cheerleader at my last school, and I'd be really good at it." I was apparently so desperate for inclusion that I was willing to dress up like a dog and fumble through techno music mash-ups at basketball games.

"Sweetie, that costume is a size medium and smells like urine. I just don't think it's going to work out for you tonight." Mrs. Rose turned off the light and ushered me out of the room with her long pink fingernails.

I waited for my mom in the dark outside the school doors, and instead of asking me how it went, she opened up the door, turned up her Carole King tape, and handed me a vanilla milk shake. We drove around in the dark, neither of us wanting to go home or talk, just like we had all my life. When my dad was screaming and out of control or she walked into our rooms crying for no good reason, she piled my brother and me in the car with ice cream and chick music and we just drove. This was her favorite coping mechanism, a tradition I proudly carry on to this day, thank you very much, Juliana Hatfield.

IT WAS INSIDE HER ALL ALONG

I entered high school at 170 pounds. As an adult I realize that I'm five foot eight and that really, in terms of proportion, 170 isn't that bad. But as a teenager, anything over 110 was basically the size of those twin fat guys on motorcycles from the *Guinness Book of World Records*. I actually shared jeans with my mother, and I'm not kidding you, guys, there are very few things as bad as that. Mariah Carey in *Glitter*. Maybe.

Supermodels were a really big thing in the nineties. I remember watching MTV one day and seeing an interview with a slew of gorgeous models, and one of the questions from the audience was what life was like for the models as kids. Pushing back tears, Tyra and Nikki and Christy justified their inhuman beauty now by explaining that as young girls, they had been absolute trolls with skinny legs and bony arms, shunned for their big teeth, towering height, and tiny waists. Then one day a switch flipped and that gap between their teeth was quirky and endearing and the gap between their legs was coveted. And I sat there in men's sweatpants thinking, *Shut the fuck up.* Tiny legs and big foreheads? That was nothing some cute bangs and flare jeans from Delia*s couldn't fix; I'd have loved to have those problems; I could work with those problems.

Much like my sisters Tyra, Nikki, and Christy, I was often teased about my looks in high school. My wavy hair was cut short and close to the scalp after an at-home blond dye job fried the ends, and I was pretty heavily into a funny T-shirt and denim overall phase. If I lingered too long at my locker or sat too close to more popular kids in class or had too much food on my tray at lunch it was as if they were obligated to keep my self-esteem in check and maintain the otherwise Stepford ecosystem of high school.

Ashley, who sat directly behind me in math class, whispered in my ear that she'd heard I'd had AIDS. I never asked who she heard that from. I don't even know anybody with AIDS. If by AIDS she meant IBS, then, yes, I had that.

Shane in art pretended the ground was shaking when I entered the classroom. I don't know for sure what he did after high school, but I'm going to assume it's becoming the world's most skillful mime, because his moves were on point.

Hannah, whom I knew from an ill-advised go on the track team, found my home number and called to tell me I was a fat whore and suggested I commit suicide after I had to give a statement to the principal about a fight she'd had with another team's shot-putter.

I became an expert at feigning illness. Colds, migraines, period cramps, diarrhea. Life lesson here, folks: nobody argues with diarrhea. Want to skip school or get out of work? Tell them you have diarrhea and can't stay out of the bathroom, and then groan a few times for effect.

By the middle of my freshman year, I had accumulated seventy-two tardies and absences, and I had begun to beg my parents to homeschool me. This was still when the only people being home-schooled were religious zealots and people with immunity problems who lived in bubbles, so the fact that I was willing to take on that societal pariah status spoke volumes. But they refused.

"You need to be in school, you need to have social interaction and friends," my mom would say.

"But you don't even see any of your friends from high school anymore," I argued.

"I didn't have a lot of friends. I was busy dating your father," she countered. "But I still see him every day, don't I?"

As a compromise, my mom told the school that we were visiting a relative out of town and pulled me out for a week. She made appointments with optometrists, dentists, and her beauty salon. I don't know if she knew the criticalness of the situation, or how badly I needed it, but it was one of the most maternal experiences I'd ever shared with my mom. Trendy clothes and cute hair might not have been important to her, but she finally sensed that they mattered to me, and she didn't protest or grimace at the cost.

I was relaunched into high school with contact lenses, the gap between my front teeth expertly filled with enamel colored bonding, and the Rachel haircut. It was life changing. Boys began respecting me and girls wanted to hang out with me. I wasn't mooed while at my locker anymore; instead I walked down the hallway confident, high-fiving my peers and laughing at all of our inside jokes. I'm just kidding; that's the plot of *She's All That,* starring Freddie Prinze Jr. and Rachael Leigh Cook. School still blew, but something did change: I got angry. Have you ever met someone who was bullied in high school and thought, *Well yeah, it sucks they are being bullied, but they're kinda a dick?* Oh, we're dicks, all right. We're dicks because we're tired of having horrible things said to us all day, of our parents not understanding, of the school not caring, and tired of having to lie down and take it until we're of legal age to move the hell away and never come back.

Until then, misery loves company, so I decided to do what all angry fat almost-feminists do: I joined the school newspaper. Maybe this would be my tribe? I'd been keeping journals for years, and in fifth grade had won an essay contest at our local library with a piece titled "My Last Six Days with Grandpa." It was a touching story about a young girl who travels to Florida to visit her grandfather, only to have him die unexpectedly. It featured a bunch of heartfelt monologues as she stood over him, reminiscing of their time together. It wasn't based on real life or anything: my grandfathers were both alive at the time, I was terrified to fly, and I have no knowledge of how to dispose of a dead human body, but nevertheless, it made the librarian cry and I was awarded first place with a laminated certificate and a pink fanny pack with Velcro. Clearly, I had the chops. Unfortunately, the only "news" the *Swanton Paw Prints* covered were random sports stories intermixed with lunch menus and gossip. My job was basically going up to groups of popular upperclassmen asking for their reactions to such hard-hitting stories as:

HEADLINE: OFFICIAL CLASS SONG POLL:
"ALL I WANNA DO" BY SHERYL CROW OR
"COTTON EYE JOE" BY REDNEX
(POPULAR ANSWER: THE NINE INCH NAILS SONG ABOUT DOING IT.)

HEADLINE: RANDO GUY IN 3RD PERIOD
CIVICS CLASS: FOREIGN EXCHANGE STUDENT,
UNDERCOVER COP, OR
CONFUSED HOMELESS MAN?

(POPULAR ANSWER: CONFUSED HOBO.
ACTUAL ANSWER: IT WAS DANIEL, A STUDENT FROM BRAZIL
WHO HAD A FULL ADULT MALE MUSTACHE.)

HEADLINE: WHY DOES THE NACHO CHEESE
TASTE WEIRD FROM THE SNACK BAR?

(POPULAR ANSWER: BLACK MOLD.)

Working for the school paper wasn't the fulfilling endeavor I'd imagined it to be. We weren't a band of intellectuals speaking up against high school injustices, and most of my ideas for controversial articles such as "Fighting Back Against Misogynist Bullies" (alternatively titled "Everyone Here Is a Bag of Dicks") were repeatedly shot down. This wasn't so much a tribe as a group of people looking to get out of English class once a week to mess around in the computer lab. After staying after class one day to resize the front-page layout to accommodate another crowdsourced fluff piece called "Smile Even Though . . ." wherein panels of my peers shared their attempts at happiness despite such first-world problems as "Smile even though . . . my parents keep picking up the phone and disconnecting the dial up modem," or "Smile even though my ex–best friends secretly three-way called me," I noticed an ad from our school choir teacher, Mrs. Zedlitz, looking to recruit chorus members for the spring musical, *The Wizard of Oz.*

Theater was something I'd secretly always wanted to try. In my elementary school's production of *Robin Hood,* I'd been cast as the understudy for the lead role . . . of Robin Hood. We actually only had four boys in our class, and Mrs. Page assured me boys played girls and girls played boys in Shakespeare all the time. The day of the play, the real Robin Hood was out with chicken pox, so I stepped into the role in a pleated dress, floral leggings, and a full beard Laura had hurriedly drawn on my face in the bathroom with a Sharpie. The beard didn't come off for a week, and Robin Hood with puberty boobs and a pleated dress was a disturbing visual, but I'd been bitten by the bug. I'd told Mrs. Page I wanted to be an actress on *Saturday Night Live* or perform on Broadway, and she shook her head and told me I'd make a great hairstylist, because I had pretty hair. That is a common chubby-girl compliment, by the way. Pretty hair and pretty faces: it's what skinny people feel safe complimenting us on when we ask if our jeans make us look fat.

"Hey, do these jeans look too tight in the leg?"

"Oh my God, Brittany, you have the best hair."

Not wanting a repeat of Cheerleading Weiner-Gate, I showed up to auditions and signed up for the chorus, because the chorus took everyone. To my surprise, I was assigned the role of an "Ozian Beautician." I wore a short green dress and sang a cute little verse about stuffing the scarecrow with new straw.

Rehearsals were going great, and I began hitting it off with other cast members. We'd laugh and joke between scenes, and meet after school to rehearse lines and gossip. As per tradition, the cast met for a group meal before the opening night, and I found myself back at our very table in Chi-Chi's eating fried ice cream and baskets of chips surrounded not by my little brother and mom, but a whole table full of friends. Everything felt full circle. Toward the end of each of the evening's performances, I stood behind the curtain backstage and watched as two skinny teenage stagehands dressed in black lowered Glenda down on a shaky white sparkly platform.

Glenda: You don't need to be helped any longer. You've always had the power to go back to Kansas.

Dorothy: I have?

Scarecrow: Then why didn't you tell her before?

Glenda: Because she wouldn't have believed me. She had to learn it for herself.

Dammit, Glenda, she was right. When I thought about what made me happy, it wasn't being liked by everyone in my class, it was being there, singing and dancing and entertaining alongside other overly dramatic people in caked-on stage makeup. Things I'd always had it in me to do, just never the confidence to try. For the first time, backstage in the auditorium at Swanton High School felt like home; it had become my tribe. I was able to channel all the angst and self-deprecation I'd spent years cultivating into something of value besides Sylvia Plath–esque journals under my bed. I began writing plays and sitcoms and telling people I wanted to be the next Carol Burnett, and they shook their heads, believing me.

By my sophomore year, I began landing lead roles. And by lead roles I mean the funny supporting lead to the much more attractive and less visually jarring main character. I often had more lines and even a few great songs, but there was always some kind of hook. Like, I had a wooden leg or a prosthetic nose or I talked like Jodie Foster in the movie *Nell,* but I had a heart of gold and a great personality. I was Eulalie Mackechnie Shinn in *The Music Man.* I was Queen Aggravain in *Once Upon a Mattress.* I auditioned and made show choir and performed dinner theater and entered state singing competitions. My confidence was sky-high.

My senior year I decided to try out for the lead in *Oklahoma!* Not the tragically slutty hillbilly cousin or the matronly old aunt, but the big one. The Shirley Jones. I had taken three months of voice lessons to beef up my soprano, and showed up to the audition wearing a maternity-cut prairie dress I'd bought at a Mennonite craft fair the next town over. To be fair, they are a surprisingly petite people, and almost all Mennonite dresses are maternity dresses.

My gay friend Casey agreed to be my audition partner, and we choreographed our scene to perfection, including the romantic kiss at the end. That was actually the hardest part; getting Casey to kiss me like I was one of the singers from Savage Garden and not like I asked him to eat bull scrotums on *Fear Factor.* We walked onstage like a totally normal heterosexual pioneer couple that had found love in windy Oklahoma and sang our hearts out. How could I not get this part? It was my moment; everything had finally come together. I was Kelly Clarkson with matte lip liner on my face, confetti raining down, winning *American Idol.*

And, I didn't get the part. At the end of evening's auditions, before I could check the callback sheet, the assistant director called me into her office, shut the door, and explained to me that I didn't get the role . . . any role, for that matter. The chemistry just wasn't there.

"I don't understand!" I cried, tears streaming down my face. "I have amazing chemistry with homosexuals. Some of my cutest boyfriends turned out to be homosexuals," I pleaded.

"It's not that." She placed her hand on my shoulder. "It's just not going to work out for you today; you just don't fit."

They gave the role of Laurey to a pretty girl named Natalie who I had been in Girl Scouts with when I was ten, until she showed me a machine gun she kept under her bed and I faked starting my period to go home. I think Casey was cast as burly Jud Fry, who, as anyone familiar with *Oklahoma!* knows, is a sexually frustrated hick who stalks around all pissed-off and rapey. Like the gay bear version of Mark Wahlberg in *Fear*.

I was offered a spot in the general chorus, but my ego couldn't take seeing someone up there in a role I had wanted so badly. It wasn't even that I particularly liked Laurey; in fact, I found the romantic lead roles to be boring and forgettable. It was more about what it represented. Here I thought I finally had the skill and talent to carry that role, despite my weight, but in the end, I just felt like a fat girl in a pregnant Amish lady dress. A month later, I was inexplicably cut from show choir, and as my world and tribe collapsed around me, I called in sick with diarrhea. Days and days of diarrhea.

It wasn't until I went off to college and sat in my seat in the auditorium for orientation that I realized nobody gave a fuck about what I'd done before that very moment. They didn't care that my dad had been hit by a truck, or that I didn't have a lot of friends, or that I'd been cut from some stupid play in high school. You didn't show up to college with some printed-off resume and accolades for your groundbreaking portrayal of Rizzo in *Grease;* you showed up wearing black and like you might have a hard-core heroin problem.

If you don't find your tribe in high school, relax; some of the best people don't. We're merely meant to make it out alive despite an oversaturated environment of both the best and worst examples of human existence, and then go on to assemble our tribes from the people we meet throwing up in bathrooms on our birthday, quoting *Caddyshack* in line at the DMV, and digging through piles of jeans at the Gap looking for the one size 18.

Until then, there is always Juliana Hatfield and ice cream.

SECRET GIRLFRIEND

THERE IS A stereotype that many overweight girls who play with Barbies into their teen years may be somewhat stunted or immature in their view of sexuality, and I am here to say . . . okay, actually I can't say anything because I have a penis in my mouth right now and am way too busy to dispute ridiculous fat person stereotypes. If anything, I always found myself to be more interested in sex than other girls my age. I hit puberty sooner, I had boobs sooner, and I even started my period sooner. I had more hormones coursing through my veins than I knew what to do with. In college I even made the ballsy decision to answer the ad in the school paper for phone sex operators because it sounded daring and exciting—also I was broke and my fridge was empty.

DO YOU HAVE A GREAT VOICE? DO YOU WANT TO WORK FROM
HOME AND MAKE YOUR OWN HOURS?

IF YOU ARE AN OPEN MINDED INDIVIDUAL WITH GREAT PEOPLE
SKILLS AND A LANDLINE TELEPHONE, YOU SHOULD JOIN OUR
TEAM OF SENSUAL EROTIC PROFESSIONALS.

*MEN, WOMEN AND PSYCHICS WANTED

During the phone interview with a southern woman named
Pam, she asked me to pretend she was a man and describe myself in
my most erotic voice.

"I'm very pale with chin-length kinky blond hair and brown
eyes," I awkwardly purred into the phone. I took her silence as a cue
to continue. "I'm wearing black underwear—I mean panties—and
I'm not wearing a bra because my boobies are so big."

"Is that you sexiest voice, hun?" she asked.

"Well, I sound more mysterious when I have a respiratory infection."

"Okay," she sighed into the receiver. "Can ya think of another
word for boobies?"

"Bosoms?"

"What about the male genitalia?"

"Like nuts?"

"Nuts?"

"Or wieners?"

Spoiler alert: I did not get the job, and saying those words out loud
was a lot harder than pointing at them in person and then putting
them inside you, which is how I handle both the majority of my fore-
play and ordering things in foreign-speaking restaurants. But what I
lacked in actual sex vocabulary, I made up for in absolute obsession,
because let's face it, sex is one of the most interesting topics in the
world. It's the basis for human life, entire channels are dedicated to
it, and wars are started because of it. The problem was that the foun-

dation of my sex obsession was built on very little factual information. I blame the Catholics.

CATHOLICS HATE VAGINAS

At the start of fourth grade I hit puberty, which is an elementary school game changer. I was what my family doctor called an "early bloomer." Nothing says, *Hey let's be friends* like me having to ask your mother for a tampon in the middle of the puppet show at your birthday party. Judy Blume had made puberty sound awesome, but Judy Blume, at least in my view, was a liar. Having boobs and hormones didn't make me mysterious and worldly; it made me lumpy and awkward in an era when the last thing I needed was more lumpy and awkward.

The classrooms of my Catholic elementary school were constructed of cement block walls and long rectangular windows, with no air-conditioning; you know, just like Jesus times. This made for summers so hot that by noon in the middle of September reaching for my hand during the Lord's Prayer in church was often met with a "Gross, why are you always so sweaty all the time?" I don't know, maybe it's because the nuns kept it hot as Nazareth in there, or that my body was racing with freaked-out hormones that made all my parts sweat and my boobs pop out awkward and pointy. I had no idea what was happening to my body, only that I was suddenly very aware of it, both because it was getting larger and because it felt different when I touched it. Puberty and sex weren't exactly topics thoroughly explained by the Catholic faith, and I certainly wasn't getting any information from my parents. In fact, the only time my father had ever spoken to me about anything related to womanhood was when I foolishly knocked on his office door to ask him what periods were after an episode of *Head of the Class.* He handed me the book *Are You There God, It's Me, Margaret,* a container of Mace, and told me my mother kept pads on the top shelf of the bathroom closet. He said menstruation was completely natural, but if I could hold off until college, that'd be great. I'm thirty now and still barely understand how periods work.

As an aside, I actually had a super-traumatic menstruation false alarm later that year after waking up in the middle of the night violently vomiting due to some questionable room-temperature ranch dressing at dinner, only to find myself also covered in blood from the waist down. Terrified, I woke my mom, who took me in the bathroom to clean me up and have a lovely conversation about how to use maxi-pads, in which I wanted to stab myself in the face. But by morning, it had become clear that our cocker spaniel, Mia, had gone into heat, and since she slept with me at night, while the puke was mine, the blood was not. I kept the pad on for the whole day anyways, just in case my person cycle aligned with Mia's dog cycle. But it didn't and my parents had Mia spayed a month later. Because waking up in the middle of the night to find a little girl with big boobs standing next to your bed covered in spoiled ranch dressing and dog period is something you never want to experience twice.

The mystery surrounding puberty and sex did nothing to stifle my curiosity; in fact, much like the overprotective moms who make you spell the words G-U-N-S and S-U-G-A-R in front of their impressionable Mensa babies only to end up raising Second Amendment–obsessed hyperglycemics, keeping it a secret terrified and excited me to the point I'd become consumed with the idea. My health teacher was increasingly uncooperative and furrowed her brown in concern each time she shook off my requests for detailed diagrams and answers about when hair would grow on my you know what, how many holes we had down there, and which ones did we put things inside of? The general takeaway from reading ahead in my health textbook was that our private parts were sacred, blood will eventually come out of them, and sex was something we weren't supposed to think about having with others or ourselves.

I didn't even know having sex with yourself was on the table until a damning revelation during my brief friendship with my atheist friend Drea, whose mother worked part-time for my parents. To Drea, I was exotic and mysterious, conducting play versions of Mass in my living room, wearing my mother's off-white silk robe, carefully placing a shortbread cookie on her tongue and blessing her as she chewed. In return for saving her from hell and relieving her from sin, Drea invited me to a sleepover with all of her public school friends. We watched PG-13 movies and drank Pepsi from two-liter bottles, until she dismissed us all to our sleeping bags, turned off the lights, and quietly instructed us on how to touch ourselves like she'd seen in the Asian pornographic movies her father collected. I didn't climax or anything, I was ten with sausage fingers and hangnails, but it felt amazing, which would go on to be a Catholic red flag. The only things Catholics are allowed to enjoy are fried cod, beer, and the movie *Sister Act*.

Later that year, before even reaching the much-anticipated section on human development and reproduction, my poor health teacher suffered an aneurysm, totally unrelated to my genital interrogations, and went to live with her sister in Florida. Health was then taken over by our priest. Father took his no-nonsense approach to crucifixion and applied it to all areas of our studies, including sex education. He split our class into a boys group and a girls group, and whichever group wasn't actively learning about sex organs got to sit in the gym and watch *Mary Poppins*.

I don't know how the boys group went, but from the time Father walked into the room, it was like we were already in trouble for something. He looked angry and impatiently tapped his foot as we took turns reading aloud about fallopian tubes and menstruation. It was like learning about the human body from the Hulk. He took no questions, and when we'd finished the chapter, he stood in front of his desk, tossed the book down, and gave it to us straight. According to the Father intercourse was a utilitarian act between a married man and woman, with the intention to make enough babies to fill a conversion van. Anything that occurred outside those specific perimeters was deemed damnable. This point was then further driven home by a ten-minute slide show of sexually transmitted diseases, followed by threats of teenage pregnancy, fiery pits of hell, and photographs of our parents and Jesus making a series of disappointed faces. None of this had been in the book.

After school that day, I went home, lay on my back against the plush pink carpet of my bedroom floor, looking up at the ceiling fan covered in dust and dog hair, and taped my vagina shut with Scotch tape.

Now, I want to say taping my vagina shut was part of a bold religious statement of empowerment, in the vein of Joan of Arc being burnt at the stake or St. Lucy of Syracuse having her eyes gouged out before execution, but the truth is that I sealed it shut out of sheer terror. The warm, electric feeling and curiosity that existed between my legs in my sleeping bag that night were replaced by shame and anxiety, and if I taped it shut, I wouldn't have to worry about accidentally touching it, or even worse yet, liking the feeling.

There were two problems with my plan, the first being that when I sat down to go to the bathroom, pee shot out of me like a clogged showerhead. The second was the ensuing rash from layers and layers of slightly urine-damp plastic tape on my labia. Three days in and I was basically dragging my crotch across the carpet like a dog until my mom grew suspicious and took me to an emergency appointment at her lady doctor. I will never forget their horrified faces as I climbed up onto the table and put my feet into the stirrups, giving them a front-row view of my swollen vagina mummified in clear sticky plastic.

Tears streamed down my cheeks as I explained to Dr. Sim and my mother what I'd learned in health class, as Dr. Sim quietly removed strip after strip of tape with long metal tweezers. I think this was the first time my mother was seeing the real-time effects of religious education, and it freaked her the fuck out. Here she thought she was getting polite, well-educated children who read at or above grade level, but the reality was that it came with a price, and that price was a daughter who put tape on her privates. Not that this should be surprising, because in general, the Catholic Church is a weird institution. Half-naked people on crosses, teen moms, Copperfield-level magic all over the place. Normal people don't emerge from that environment.

I left that office with my very first scheduled therapy appointment, instructions to apply the steroid cream until the redness and swelling subsided, and an inflatable hemorrhoid pillow to use until the skin grew back.

In case you ever catch yourself wondering just how judgmental small children can be, ask the girl in fourth grade who had to sit on a hemorrhoid pillow because her labia was full of scabs.

"My mom said that putting stuff on your private parts gets you on sex offender lists."

"You're not a sex offender if you put tape on your own privates, Tara," I shot back.

Just when I thought they'd never let me live that shit down, two weeks later a boy in my class went up to the chalkboard to answer a math problem with an erection. Nobody really remembered I taped my vagina shut after that. Thank God for erections, am I right?

SHE GIVES IT ALL AWAY

An issue many overweight women face is that it's very easy to have a great deal of your womanhood and femininity robbed from you. You aren't a possible mate because you aren't pretty; instead you're just "like a sister" or "one of the guys" or Madonna's wingman in *A League of Their Own*. Once I had enough distance between myself and Catholic school, and the scars on my vagina had healed, I began to search out a point of connection between the girlishness and attractiveness I wasn't feeling, and that connection became messing around with boys. Or in bitter high school girl terms, I became a huge whore, which was actually somewhat of a challenge because I looked like a fat Dutch Boy with boobs.

As it should come to the surprise of no one, I had very little experience with boys. My first French kiss was with my neighbor named Grant while playing spin the bottle with him and my brother in his parents' basement. Honestly, there were very few good outcomes in that game.

So, I depended heavily on my friends to help me wade through the waters of boys and relationships. Typically, there were two ways to ask out a guy. If you were confident he was going to say yes, you did it yourself at his locker or between classes. If the potential outcome was fuzzy, you sent your friend in to do it like a shady used car salesman.

"Sure she looks a little rough around the edges, but under that ear zit and faint mustache, she really purrs."

That approach panned out for me only one time, with my very first boyfriend, Vince. Vince was a quiet boy with curly hair that fell into his eyes, and a complete stoner. My cousin Parris asked him out for me while we were at a party. He was sitting at the dining room table lighting napkins on fire with his Zippo lighter, when she whispered in his ear and pointed at me from across the room. He shrugged, said yes, and we spent the next hour kissing in the woods next to a rusted-out VW bus. Having never had a boyfriend before, I relished all the intricacies of our relationship. Like the way he fingered me in the movie theater during *Natural Born Killers.* Or wrote me poems about death, but in a really romantic way like, *won't it be awesome when we're both dead and we can be two rotting corpses in the same grave hole for all of eternity or until they bulldoze out our remains to build a Walmart?*

It's a cliché to say I was in love, but I truly thought I was. Until three months later when Vince dumped me on my birthday for a girl in Georgia who was technically his third or fourth cousin. I can't be sure if those crazy kids ever made it, but if they did, you can bet there's a handful of gorgeous curly-haired inbred children running around somewhere with two different-colored eyes and an anus coming out of their foreheads.

Outside of Vince, which I think we can all agree was a major bullet dodged, the remainder of my time as an underclassman was spent being a secret girlfriend. Secret girlfriends were not the same as pretend girlfriends. We weren't made-up girls you never see because we lived in Canada or only proved our existence through naked pictures shared in AOL chat rooms. Secret girlfriends were girls who had legitimate relationships with boys, even though nobody else was around to verify it was actually happening. The males in my school, who so often never gave me a passing sexual thought, soon realized that with soft stomachs and thick thighs come large boobs. Suddenly I was spending a lot of time with boys who were too ashamed to be seen with me in public, either because of what I looked like, or the fact that they already had other more attractive nonsecret girlfriends who were often busy every weekend at track meets or volleyball games. They'd pick me up on Friday nights and we'd drive to empty parking lots or back to their homes if their parents were gone. We'd start out watching movies on the couch, but would always end up making out for a few hours before they'd realized how late it had gotten, usher me back to the car, and drive me back home stone-faced and stoic. Now that the sexual urge had been filled, all that was left for them was regret. If there was one constant in this part of my life, it was that they never kissed me goodbye, not once.

And yet, it wasn't until the light of day, or at least by the light of the fluorescent bulbs that lined the aging school hallways from 8 A.M. and 2:20 P.M., as those same boys who breathed my name into my neck as they fumbled with the hooks of my bra walked past me not meeting my eyes, that I remembered this wasn't a real relationship.

I know, I know, it's really easy for me to look back at this from my self-esteem high horse and cringe. But this was a different time. Clinton was president. We were still eating gluten. The

9/11 attacks hadn't happened yet. I didn't know I was doing a disservice to chubby girls everywhere; I was more focused on the fact that when I was making out with a boy in a car in the woods I felt like a girl for the very first time. Being heavy *and* wanted was a completely new concept; it never dawned on me that I had a say in all this, or that I had the right to be picky about who I allowed access to my body. I was just thankful someone, anyone, had wanted it.

And they could have it, as much of it that they'd like, except for sex. It might sound arbitrary considering, but sex was something I held tight to. Not for religious reasons, or even fear, though being terrified of your first time was completely normal, but more out of self-preservation and control. I may not have been able to change the way I looked, or my station in life at that moment, but I could control who got my virginity. I would give it away when it felt right, and so far, being left standing in my driveway as upperclass-man boys pulled away popping gum in their mouths and covering my scent with Calvin Klein's Obsession before they met up with their real girlfriends didn't feel right.

My journals in high school read like the playbook of a plus-size Donna Martin from *90210*. Like Donna, I was not only saving myself, but was self-conscious about my nose and had two different-sized breasts.

NOVEMBER 1996

I gave Grant a blowjob in his car after school, again. Yes, that Grant. The Grant who took me on one date before leaving me at the restaurant while I was in the bathroom, and his friend Tom had to drive me home. I have no idea what my problem is, he barely acknowledges me in school or at play practice. I swear to God he looks like he fell out of the show Felicity with his puka shell necklaces, layers of sweaters and flannel shirts, and worn looking

Dr. Martens. It's like he walks around to a perpetual soundtrack of Mazzy Star's "Fade Into You." I saw him talking to Emily at her locker, which makes absolutely no sense, because Emily is incredibly boring and has a haircut like Frasier, but when we talked on the phone last night he promised he doesn't even like Emily, his mom wanted him to date her, but he totally isn't going to. He also asked me to come over this weekend when his parents are gone to watch movies and said to be sure to wear a skirt. He probably wants me to dress up for when he asks me to Homecoming.

Grant didn't ask me to homecoming, and he only wanted me to wear a skirt because it was the nineties and those button-fly jeans were a complete pain in the ass.

FEBRUARY 1997

There are perks to living across the street from a senior boy. Like when he and his friends show up to your house drunk on a weekend night and ask if you have any beer. One of the guys, Beau, who is totally Grant's best friend by the way, yes that Grant who left me at a Big Boy restaurant and took boring Emily to Homecoming, is beyond hot. Beau is dating a senior girl named Sarah, but he said I was much prettier and that Sarah was too busy with sports to mess around on the weekends. I have spent the last two months' worth of Saturdays with Beau, and he can't wait until track is over so he can break up with Sarah. He's not doing it yet because she's going to state and totally doesn't want to break her concentration because that wouldn't be fair to her, plus he really likes hanging out with her dad. The other day Beau and I were making out in my parents' barn, and he stuck his finger so far up inside me, I started bleeding. He wasn't even grossed out. Beau is so much sweeter than Grant.

Beau never broke up with Sarah; in fact, he married her.

Big news, a local celebrity was in my house tonight! Pete was all over the local paper for bowling that perfect game, and after being my partner in art class for the screen printing project, he finally asked to come over and hang out. We kissed on my bed, and then he showed me his thumb, which was disgusting. Apparently if you spend a few years sticking your thumbs into bowling balls, they turn into deformed lightbulbs covered in calluses and dandruff. He asked me if I wanted to watch him bowl in a tournament the next weekend. Obviously, I said yes. Then about an hour after Pete left he three-way called me with a girl named Julia who said she worked at the bowling alley and was dating him. She called me a fat whore and a nasty pig, and then made Pete tell me that he loved only her and then they hung up on me. I have no idea why she was so angry at me; I wasn't cheating on my girlfriend. Every time my mom asks me when Pete is coming back over, I feel like a bigger idiot. I'm not introducing anyone to her again.

And then Pete failed out of high school and went to jail. I feel like way less of an idiot now.

Tonight at Show Choir practice John cornered me in the Choir room and asked me if I'd be interested in 69'ing. I didn't even know what that was; he had to draw it out for me on a paper plate. I told him I would think about it, leaning over someone while my stomach hangs down isn't exactly a flattering position for me. Also, John has been giving me really weird vibes. I mean, he is a great soccer player and has an amazing body, but when we hang out he makes me give him a hand job by standing behind him, and then he asked me to bulk up my legs and shoulders because he said girls were sexier that way.

John ended up joining the navy after high school and now he lives in Chicago with his husband, Brett, who probably doesn't have to stand behind him while giving hand jobs. I'm on their Christmas card list.

FEELS LIKE THE FIRST TIME

I officially lost my virginity at seventeen to a boy named Andy in the back of his car to the Tears for Fears song "Shout." I say officially because I used to ride horses and I was really aggressive with tampons so whatever was left of my hymen was probably like crossing the finish line second behind the guy who already broke the ribbon. It wasn't even his idea, it was mine. I knew I had wanted to give it to him, it had finally felt right.

Andy and I had both attended the yearly trip to Mexico our Spanish Club took, and after a night of discotheques and cheap sugary liquor, I asked him in the hallway of our hotel if he wanted to have sex with me. He said no.

"No?" I repeated, stunned and dizzy leaning against the damp wallpaper.

"No, not like this," he explained.

I never asked him why; the last thing I wanted to be was the girl who had to beg a boy to sleep with her. So I let it go for the rest of the trip and instead focused on underage drinking and catchy Will Smith songs. Honestly, I have no idea why my parents thought it was a good idea to let me go on a vastly underchaperoned trip to Cancún. Children, if you are reading this, you are never going to Mexico.

I'm not entirely sure what Mexico lacked in ambience, but there I was three months later, same Andy, different country. We were parked in a wooded area behind my parents' house, having sex in the passenger-side seat of his dented Honda hatchback. It was awkward and sloppy and lasted about five minutes. When we were finished tears began to gather in the corner of my eyes, not out of pain or regret, but of relief. I looked up at him breathing heavily above me, holding himself up by the strength of his arms on either side of my seat.

I'd gone to Victoria's Secret the day before and told the clerk I was buying lingerie for my slutty older sister's bachelorette party. I explained that we were roughly the same size, but she was insecure about her nipples being too large, so nothing see-through. I left with a black baby doll chemise and some crotchless matching panties that I'd hidden beneath the loose jeans and a Charlotte Hornets Starter jacket that now sat bunched on the floor of the car.

"What's wrong?" he asked alarmed. He had been growing out a mustache and it was the most ridiculous thing I had ever seen.

"I feel like a girl right now," I admitted, laughing up at the gray felt ceiling of the car.

"I hope so," Andy answered. "Because I definitely saw at least one pussy down there." I cringed at the word, but forgave him.

We both found our places back in our seats and re-dressed in silence. He put his car in reverse and drove me back down the bumpy dirt road to my house. I had sex with a boy who would go on to take me prom, introduce me to his parents, and never leave me at a restaurant when I wasn't looking. So many of my skinny, gorgeous friends have absolutely horrible stories about losing their virginity, and aside from an unfortunate eighties song about the Cold War, my first time was perfect.

As I reached for the handle on the car door to get out, Andy put his hand on my arm stopping me, leaned forward, and kissed me goodbye for the very first time.

MY ANDY GIBBONS

I CAN'T REALLY talk about anything else before first talking about Andy Gibbons. I'm going to be mentioning him a lot going forward, and it's rude not to introduce someone properly. Like those people who tell you stories about their family by saying, "Oh, did I mention Mom was in the hospital?" And I respond like "What!? I thought Mom was in her living room watching *Deadliest Catch*!" Because we actually don't have the same mom, and it's weird to assume we do, because we look nothing alike and we just met. It's called a possessive determiner and it helps me not freak out about my mom being in the hospital.

I met Andy Gibbons, *my* Andy Gibbons, on his birthday. While we attended the same school and had a few mutual friends, I had absolutely no idea who Andy was, and at that point was really only hanging out with boys who were gay or ashamed to be seen with me.

On April 5, Andy turned sixteen, passed his driver's test, loaded up three of his friends into the black 1988 Honda hatchback he inherited from his older brother, and spent the celebratory afternoon driving around and listening to rap music. I met him three hours later when he knocked on my front door and asked to use my phone. (It's weird to think we didn't have cell phones back then. We just left the house untethered, assuming we'd eventually show back up in one piece. Now I can't even sit at a red light and not check my iPhone. The one time I left home without it, I tried to use the pay phone at the gas station, but when I picked it up, the part you spoke into had been removed and the hole stuffed with used condoms. The fact that there were multiple condoms in there confused me; I wasn't sure if someone was having regular sex into the speaker hole, or if it was the work of a really horny squirrel.)

Andy needed to use my telephone because he had been in an accident in front of my house, and while physically okay, he needed to call his mother. I gave him our cordless phone and went to the kitchen to get him a glass of water since it seemed like the polite thing to do for someone who had just been in a car accident. I was relieved my parents were both at work that day so I could corral all the dogs into their bedroom at the back of the house, muffling their barking and whining at the door. When he later recounted this series of events to his buddies, I didn't want him referring to me as the weird girl who had a hundred dogs in her house.

Andy looked terribly young. Tall and thin with thick messy black hair covering his pale blue eyes, and acne along his jaw. He wore a basketball jersey as a shirt, a gold Nike swoosh necklace, and his baggy jeans appeared to be ironed. I sat down next to him on the cement of our front porch and listened as he explained to his mom on the phone that a car had tried to pass him as he was turning, and T-boned him into my front yard. His voice was shaky, but he assured her he was fine and that he'd need a ride home.

He hung up and we sat together stiffly.

"Hi, I'm Brittany," I said, extending my hand to his.

"I know who you are," he said, raising his eyebrows. "We're in the same class."

Andy clenched his jaw and looked straight ahead as the tow truck driver raised his car onto the platform. I had nothing in common with him, and frankly, I wanted him to leave. It was rare I got the house to myself, and I was dying to get back to Eric Nies and MTV's *The Real World*.

A short while later, a silver sedan pulled into our long wooded driveway. Andy stood up, thanked me for the water and letting him use my phone, got into his mom's car, and left. Just like that. And that, children, is how I met your father.

The next morning I awoke to the sound of dogs barking, a collective hounding that occurred whenever anyone dared to ring our doorbell or knock. I spent a large portion of my time in that house trying to beat visitors to the front door in hopes of heading off the barking and visitors giving looks of animal hoarding concerns. After a few minutes had passed my dad gently rapped on my bedroom door, stuck his head in, and said, "Uh, there's an Andy Gibbons here to see you?" My puzzled expression matched his, and I hurriedly grabbed the bra from my floor and strapped it on underneath my plaid pajama shirt.

I found Andy sitting calmly with my mother in the living room, on our brown floral couch, buried underneath a cocker spaniel and two Great Danes.

"Hi, um, Andy, right?" I stammered. There was a stranger in my living room with my mother. "Did you forget something or do you need a statement for the police or something?"

"Nah, I actually came over to see if you wanted to go to breakfast?" he asked, pushing the panting dogs from his lap as he stood up.

"I am still in my pajamas." Because holy shit, I was still in my pajamas, and not even cute ones. An oversize plaid nightshirt from the women's section of Sears that had two large vertical holes in the chest that, I assumed, were for scratching your boobs through; only later would I realize it was a nursing nightgown.

"That's fine, I was just going to go to the McDonald's drive-through and drive around town while we ate."

"I don't know, I usually don't eat in front of people and I don't know anything about you aside from the fact that you are a terrible driver."

My mother, clearly just excited there was a straight nonrelative boy in the house, pushed me off into my room to change. I once saw this woman show up to a funeral in Crocs and a Looney Tunes shirt, and suddenly she was Mrs. Bennet prettying me up for Mr. Darcy. I threw on a hoodie and a pair of cutoff jean shorts and climbed into the silver Nissan his mother had been driving a day earlier.

"Nice car," I offered, running my hand along the soft leather and fancy buttons.

"Thanks." He smiled. "Mine's in the shop."

We drove around quietly sipping orange juices and listening to the lyrical stylings of Dr. Dre. Every so often he would point to the house of a friend or ask me a question about my life.

"So did your mom just find all those dogs?"

"No, she breeds them, so we have that many on purpose," I answered, looking out the window.

We drove along the old railroad track and down country roads past fields and grazing livestock.

"Do you watch many movies?" I asked, hoping to have some noise drown out whatever was happening through the speakers.

"No. I am busy with basketball and golf, and I play lots of video games."

"Wow, that sounds awesome." I sighed, bored out of my mind.

"Hey did your parents make you take me out to breakfast as a thank-you or something, because this really isn't necessary."

"No." He laughed. "I asked you to breakfast because you make me nervous and I can't stop thinking about yesterday with your hair piled all up on your head in that messy bun thing. I just keep sitting there on your porch wanting to kiss you."

"Well, that's unfortunate." My faced burned and I felt an actual shift inside my body, as if room were suddenly being made to accommodate all the feelings that were bouncing around in my stomach between the Egg McMuffin and hash browns. "I don't kiss boys who listen to rap music."

And that was actually true. My mom's best friends were her partners in the dog show circuit, Mike and Casey. Casey did the grooming, Mike did the showing, and my mom turned our attached garage into a working kennel. I loved tagging along with her to their home in southern Michigan, because while she and Mike, a hairy Greek man who reminded me of a character from *Taxi,* talked business, I got to hang out with Casey. Casey was in his forties with a receding hairline and thin mustache. He wore kimonos around the house, offered me hand-rolled cigarettes, and had a giant white cockatoo that cursed in French and drank scotch from a lowball glass. He also gave the absolute best life advice, and loved gossiping with me about the mean girls in my school, which was exciting, because usually fat girls don't get their gay best friends until they try to turn them straight in college.

"Between you and me," he'd whisper, leaning in, shaking the ice around in his glass as we sat cross-legged on the long white leather couches of his living room, "Andrea sounds like a giant cunt, and if I were you, I'd tell her that right to her face."

"Oh sweetie, you don't want to be homeschooled," he'd coo to me as I'd cry on the phone at ten o'clock on a school night. "Home-schooling is for trolls and people who start churches with only their family as members; you have so much potential and great eyebrows."

"Chubby girls have great boobs. Have your mom buy you a bra with an underwire instead of this elastic undershirt crap from the k .d. lang collection," he'd quip before storming out of the mall dressing room full of ill-fitting homecoming dresses.

And it was from Casey that I received perhaps some of the greatest relationship rules ever.

1 Never date a boy who listens to rap music and makes you call him by his white rapper name.
2 If the first kiss is bad, the second will be way worse.
3 A good night cream is more important than air.
4 Nothing saves a Keanu Reeves movie except a well-timed hand job.
5 Hickeys are for truck drivers with jealous wives.
6 If a boy tells you he is gay, believe him, believe him, believe him.

At the red light at Main Street and Cherry, I broke rule number one. And a few months later, rule number four, but to be fair, *A Walk in the Clouds* was a really lame movie.

CITY MOUSE FAT COUNTRY MOUSE

I was Andy's first real girlfriend, so bringing me home to meet his parents was a big deal. He lived in a pretty brick home on a wooded street uptown. Not that Swanton was a metropolis, but there was marked difference between the people who lived in town with lawn service and access to city water, and we country folk who got our water from underground wells and mowed our lawns with actual tractors. Dressing for this experience was hard, as his family was decidedly fancier than my own. His father worked in IT and his mother in real estate. I hadn't seen her since the day she'd picked him up from my house after the accident, but she drove a new car and had a vanity license plate, two things I equated with very rich people.

I had saved my babysitting money to buy a cute men's red plaid windbreaker from the Gap, and was going through a phase where I wore it with everything, no matter the weather. If it was hot, I pulled it over my head with shorts and brown leather sandals. If it was cold, I wore it with jeans and platform shoes. I rationalized this by thinking I looked thinner hiding my midsection and arms beneath an oversize men's jacket, and so showed up to his front door in a pair of khaki shorts, leather clogs, and my signature plaid windbreaker.

"You must be Brittany." His mother greeted me with a smile. She was tall with whitish blond hair cut into a perfectly smooth bob. She stepped aside opening the glass door so I could walk in.

"It's so nice to finally meet you." I beamed with my friendliest grin, accepting her pale thin hand in a handshake.

"Andy's just in the living room. Here, let me take your jacket and you can go on in," she said, her arms outstretched for my coat.

"Oh, that's okay," I said, deflecting her offer. "It's chilly and I'll keep it on awhile longer."

"Are you sure? It's at least eighty degrees and we're eating outside," she pressed.

"I'm sure, I . . ." I paused, thinking of a plausible reason to be wearing a large canvas coat in the middle of summer. "I'm not wearing anything underneath it," I answered.

She stared at me puzzled, tilting her head to one side the way dogs do when they hear a new noise. I walked past her, mortified, to find Andy smiling on the couch, suddenly worried at my red face and rapid breathing.

"Is everything okay?" he whispered as I sat down beside him on the long white sofa.

"Super okay," I lied. "I'm so happy to be here."

We had dinner on the sunporch, ignoring the formal dining room table that was perpetually set with full china and stemware. His parents asked me about school and what classes I enjoyed. I talked about the musicals I had performed in and the part-time job I held busing tables at the local Mexican cantina. Beads of sweat ran down my back as Andy and his father talked about golf and the latest electronics. I smiled and followed along, every so often playing with the hair I'd spent an hour straightening that was now frizzy and wet underneath. It wasn't that his parents weren't welcoming; it was more that the welcome felt temporary. I was okay as a girlfriend, for now. But as they talked about upcoming trips they were taking and Andy going off to college the next year, it became clear that beyond this moment, there would be no room for me.

Andy walked me to the white Ford Taurus I'd borrowed from my mom, and kissed me as I leaned against the driver's-side door.

"So, are you really naked under this jacket?" he asked, slowly pulling up the bottom hem.

"No." I swatted at his hand. "I didn't know what to say. I'm so embarrassed. I can't believe she told you." I buried my face into his shoulder.

From that point on, we spent the majority of our time at my house. Not because his parents banned me from their home after allegedly showing up naked under a jacket like some sort of French hooker, but because I needed another place to feel uncomfortable like I needed a hole in my head. My parents were burly and my house crowed and unkempt, but I was used to the noise, and when I was there, I didn't feel like I didn't fit in.

About a year into our relationship, as my father lumbered out of the bathroom in his high-waisted underwear I turned to ask Andy for the thousandth time, "Seriously, why do you like me, again?" And he would laugh, brush the Great Dane hair and slobber from his nicely pressed Izod shirt, and kiss me.

As much as our lives had nothing in common, Andy and I shared a common desire: we both wanted out. Andy, from the shadow of his brother, ten years his senior, who set the precedent for high grades, college scholarships, and a successful military career. Me, from being the primary mental caretaker of two sometimes suicidal parents and revolving brood of six to ten dogs. Many of our dates consisted of us lying together on the wobbly wooden deck of the broken-down aboveground pool in my backyard, looking up at the stars, smoking a joint, and talking about leaving home.

"My brother joined the air force in college," he'd tell me. "Now he lives on base in Colorado Springs in a free house with his wife."

"That sounds perfect," I'd answer, not really sure if this vision included me or not.

"You wouldn't even have to work if you didn't want to." He said this with a smile, answering the question that hung in the air above our heads. I couldn't tell if it was because he made me feel beautiful or because I knew he was going to help me leave; either way, I loved him.

"I love you, you know," I said staring up at the sky, the words coming out too high and shaky, making my ears ring as I said them.

"Really?" he asked, rolling up on his side to look at me.

"Yes," I sighed, staring into his ice-blue eyes and pushing the shaggy black hair out of his face.

"Well I love you, too." He smiled.

"Good," I answered, sitting up, "because I wasn't going to give you your first blow job unless you said it back."

"Uh, it's your first, too, right?" he asked, his voice fast and nervous.

"Does it really matter?" I asked as I unzipped his jeans and sank my head down low into his lap.

"Not anymore," he moaned, letting his head fall back onto the damp wood of the deck, covering his face with his hands.

And really, who wants to be the person someone learns to give their first blow job on, anyway?

6

COLLEGE, I DON'T KNOW WHY I'M HERE, EITHER?

THE WORST DECISION I ever made was to go to college.

In my head, I totally imagined myself getting some sort of honorary doctorate and having my student loans wiped cleaned based on the success of this book, but fuck it, I'm going to keep this real. Don't go to college. It's the absolute worst and it will ruin your life and you'll never have good enough credit to own things, ever. Learn a trade or invent Facebook. College is for dummies.

When I'm asked to speak at a high school or event, I always try to open with this little nugget of wisdom, but the organizers shut me down, all *yeah this feels like maybe it's the incorrect message to spread to young people.*

Let's try this again: if you decide to go to college, which is fine because I'm not the boss of you and you can do what you want, even if what you want is to make really stupid financial decisions, know that it's totally okay to have no idea what you want to do once you get there. In fact, college or not, that's a general life rule. You are allowed to float around having no damned idea what you want to do with yourself, with no actual time frame in which you need to figure it out. People like your parents or your boyfriend, will act like you have a time frame, but it's all a ruse to get you to move out of your bedroom or pay your share of the rent. Take your time. Just remember this: college is the most expensive place to be confused in the whole entire world.

> *Congratulations! We are delighted to offer you admission to The Ohio State University for Fall 1999 as a Freshman. Your hard work and determination have earned you a spot in The Ohio State University Class of 2004! Since admission to The Ohio State University is a selective process, you should take pride in this accomplishment.*

In accordance with the plan of Andy and me to leave our hometown and never come back, I applied and was accepted into The Ohio State University, a Big Ten college located in Columbus, Ohio. It's one of the country's largest schools; I went from a graduating class of 120 to over sixty thousand. I'm going to pause here in case you are a Buckeyes fan, because I can already feel you getting giddy and spazzy on the edge of your seat waiting for me to bellow "O-H" in your direction, so *O-H!*

If you are not a Buckeyes fan, whether it's because you don't follow college football or you think our team is made up of a bunch of cheating, overrated criminals, forget I said anything.

Now, I don't want to sound all small-town beauty pageant right here, but at the time, getting accepted into college was pretty amazing. I was the first in my family to go, and one of only a handful of members of my graduating class moving away. Putting aside that I was playing the insecure-girlfriend card when I decided to attend the same college as my boyfriend, I was pretty proud of myself for my accomplishment, and things started off great. I had a cute dorm room on the south campus and was assigned a perfectly normal roommate named Sarah. At that time Sarah was majoring in Spanish and dating a migrant farmworker named Arron (you have to roll the *rr* when you say it) who spoke no English and sat stoically on her twin bed and stared at me while I studied. I couldn't figure out if he hated me or was genuinely curious of my American ways. Sarah told me he had some disorder that made him sleep with his eyes open, so it wasn't that he didn't like me, he was just napping.

I began my college career majoring in early childhood education, because in my head, I liked kids. Also, every career aptitude test I took in high school came up inconclusive. I was actually fired from my first job as a busgirl at a Mexican restaurant after my thirty-day review, in which I was described as "aloof, distracted, and bad at carrying things like glasses or sharp knives." I was lacking direction and working with small children seemed like a fun job, until I volunteered at a local homeless shelter near campus. While playing hot potato with a group of kids, the adorable little girl I was holding turned around and threw up into my open mouth.

I immediately stood up, rinsed my face off in the sink, and ran to the Student Health Center demanding to be tested for every disease in existence, not because she was homeless, but because another human being had vomited into my mouth. I feel the need to clarify that point. I just walk around assuming all people who are *not me* have infectious diseases and contagious open sores, whether they are homeless or not.

The next day I went to the arts and sciences department to switch my major to Undecided, but opted at the last minute to go with English, which my school advisor explained as being basically the same thing.

A SERIES OF BLIND DATES

I was lucky early on in that my college advisor, Jemma, realized I was a bit of a flight risk, and decided to help pave the way to my future adult career using glossy brochures and fancy metaphors.

"Think of internships as career blind dates," she said excitedly.

Jemma felt that the best way for me to actually figure out if I wanted to do something for the rest of my life was to nibble on it for eight to ten weeks before realizing it tasted like an old diaper and then lighting it on fire and watching it burn to the ground. Which happens to be how all seven of my internships ended, by the way.

Event planner. My first internship was for a nonprofit agency that was planning its yearly fund-raising event at a downtown art gallery. Throwing parties for a living seemed like a dream job, and how else to guarantee being invited, than to be the one making the list? The night of the event I spent fourteen hours in heels yelling at caterers and band directors, all the while being berated through a tiny Britney Spears headset by a small Australian woman named Natasha. The only fun I had that night was after the guests left and I smoked pot with the Mexican kitchen staff out back. I asked them if they knew Arron (you have to roll the *rr* when you say it), and they did not.

Lawyer. I got this internship at the height of popularity of *The Practice,* when plus-size powerful women in smart suits were a thing—high-five Camryn Manheim. The red flag should have been that every young lawyer I encountered in the firm silently mouthed the words "Do Not Go to Law School" to me from their shared offices, but it wasn't until I experienced how inherently boring real court hearings were and that nobody actually looked like Dylan McDermott that I realized I couldn't do this for the rest of my life.

Reporter. The summer after my sophomore year in college I scored an internship as a summer reporter for a local ABC News affiliate. I was really excited to have been chosen for this opportunity. I mean, who doesn't want to be famous and on television? So, okay, fine, I wasn't actually on camera, but the people I held the microphone up to as I asked questions didn't know that. To them, I was a fancy TV reporter. My excitement began to dull after a few weeks of writing copy aimed at the lowest common denominator, with absolutely no artistic license.

John, the anchor: This weekend Worthington is hosting their third annual community dog wash in the park. I guess they don't call it the dog days of summer for nothing.

Shannon, the other anchor: Oh John, you are hilarious.

I was eventually "fired" after I forgot to bring a pen with me to interview the manager of McDonald's about the exciting new launch of bratwurst, so the only note I took was writing "McWeiners" on my notepad in eyeliner. According to my supervisor, you can't be serious about news without a pen.

Radio DJ. I actually really loved this job. I worked on a morning radio show, and the main hosts were crude and funny. Having an internship at a radio station was like showing up every day to a game of Truth or Dare; I was able to write funny bits and was rewarded for pranks and general debauchery. It also did wonders for my self-esteem as my coworkers spent their time on the clock wearing pajamas and eating fast food. Unfortunately for me, the consensus was that I didn't have an interesting enough dialect for radio and that nobody wants to live in a world where every other song I played is by Hall & Oates.

Public relations. I thought that PR meant working for a band or celebrity, but in Ohio, working in public relations meant putting a pretty face on a local metal manufacturer who might or might not be destroying Earth and killing polar bears with pollutants. Also, being in public relations isn't a good choice if the person who is having a meltdown is usually you.

Newspaper columnist. I get genuinely sad when I think about the dying industry that is print news. Sure it's dated and irrelevant, but seeing your byline in print is a surreal life experience, even if your byline happens to be in the obituaries section. Side note: lots of people die in farm machinery accidents in Ohio. *Deadliest Harvest.* How is there not a Discovery show about this yet?

Jemma sat at her desk perplexed. I'd spent a year and two summer quarters trying on different jobs, and none of them felt like home. I think we both began to wonder if the issue was the job, or just my poor work ethic.

"What do you want to do," she asked. "Right now."

"Write a book. Be on *Saturday Night Live.* Maybe meet Bill Murray," I answered confidently.

"Yes, but these aren't things you go to college for," Jemma explained. Finally we were on the same page.

"I know. I don't know why I'm here, either."

Finally the truth was out. I'd followed a boy here and wanted to get away from my parents so badly that I'd taken out tens of thousands of dollars in student loans to do it. But Jemma was determined and began pensively clicking around her computer screen.

"How do you feel about politics?" she asked, twirling a black braid between her fingers.

"Al Gore is really hot and I'm pro-choice?"

"Perfect, the state capitol is hiring interns for the House," she explained. "There are a few Democrat openings; wanna try it?" She blinked at me expectantly.

YOU CAN CALL ME MONICA, IF YOU WANT TO

The names in this section have been omitted because I don't feel like being murdered by the Secret Service.

When I reached the designated floor of the Ohio Statehouse, the elevator doors opened to a sign reading "Majority" and pointing to the left down a beautifully painted corridor with gold-framed pictures of old men, satin couches with fluffy throw pillows, and vases of flowers on every table.

Below that sign was a plaque that read "Minority," and which pointed to the hallway to the right, which looked nothing like the majority's entryway, but instead resembled the kind of third-world hostel you see in documentaries about people being kidnapped and sold as sex slaves. I rechecked the wrinkled Post-it in my hands.

The Representative. Ask for Maggie.

I made my way down the dimly lit hallway until it opened to a large wooden desk manned by a small young woman with brown curly hair and cat eye glasses.

"You must be Brittany." She stood enthusiastically. "I'm Maggie, the Representative's executive assistant."

Maggie showed me around the offices, introducing me to various levels of assistants and assistant assistants and filling me in on political gossip. Our half of the floor was a maze of gray cubicles emitting a low murmur of tired voices in cheap business suits, answering phone calls and typing nonsense into decade-old technology. It was moist and depressing, and where I would be spending my entire spring quarter.

She walked me to my cubicle, which was a bit of a shithole, literally. Across the fuzzy inner walls it had brown stains that resembled feces or dried blood. I don't want to think about what might have gone down in there before I started. Maggie explained how to work the phone system and the computer. Due to my class schedule, I was coming in during the afternoons, so the majority of my work would take place after the other staffers had left and the phones were shut off, but my primary tasks were to take and document constituent calls, open and sort the mail, and put the day's files away.

"Will I get a chance to meet the Representative?" I asked. After all, wasn't that why I was here, to see if being him was awesome?

"Oh no, he isn't around in the afternoons. He's here in the morning, then that's it. Lots of meetings and hearings to attend," she chirped, and then double-checking that I was okay, left me to get settled.

Weeks passed, and the only glimpse I got of the Representative was from the framed pictures in his office as I dropped the armfuls of mail on his desk. He was a tall black man, somewhat heavyset, with sad, dark eyes, a thick graying mustache, and huge hands. He'd met President Clinton and dined with world leaders and beauty queens.

The intern work was boring and uneventful, starting off each day with a hefty bout of constituent calls regarding property line disputes, unfilled potholes, and rising crime crates, finishing off my time by opening hundreds of pieces of mail, sorting it into piles based on importance, and distributing it accordingly. Running America was monotonous.

"You know what, Mrs. Miller, I can take a message on that, but the local government actually has very little say in who wins Top Chef."

"No, Mr. Lords, Ohio has no concrete plans to secede from the Union at this time. But I will absolutely take a message."

"I agree, Mr. Perez, your neighbor sounds like a total jerk. Now, is the dick he's spray painting on your privacy fence an actual penis or just the word *dick,* and yes, it matters."

When I was sure everyone had gone home for the day, I'd sneak into the representative's office to open and sort mail from the comfort of his giant mahogany desk and cool leather spinny chair. The floor was stuffy and humid, and the air-conditioning in his office was a welcome relief from the sweat and smell so I made myself at home next to a picture of him playing basketball with some old white guy and chatted with my mom on speakerphone, because it was mid-month and I'd long since drank away all my cell phone bill money. It was during a particularly passionate retelling of the *Sex and the City* finale when the representative walked into his office wearing a black tuxedo under a long black trench coat.

"Oh my God." I hit the button on speakerphone and jumped up from the chair.

"Who is Mr. Big, Miss Buckenmeyer?" he asked. His voice was low and paced, and when he spoke it felt like velvet fabric slowly slipping between my fingers. Suddenly my hands went numb and my heart started beating against the inside of my rib cage. I couldn't tell if I was having an actual panic attack or my body was just shutting down out of fear. I don't actually have the "flight" part of the fight-or-flight reflex. Come to think of it, I don't even have the fight part. I have whatever emergency reflex causes my knees to stop working and my bladder to release. I just fold down like those tiny wooden Push Puppet toys and pee.

"Mr. Big was—*is* a lobbyist." I answered. Why couldn't I feel my lips? Was my mouth even working correctly? Was saliva just sliding out the corners?

He stood stone-faced, taking up the doorway with his immense shoulders. Even if I had the ability to active my "flight" sense, it would have been useless. He didn't speak or even flinch. He just looked at me calmly, as I fidgeted with the pencil skirt I'd half unzipped after eating the chicken club out of the snack room vending machine, and looked down to realize I'd left my shoes kicked off under his desk.

I covered my face with my hands in defeat. Fucking Carrie Bradshaw. "He's not a lobbyist. I am so sorry, sir. I thought everyone had gone for the day, and it's so hot in my cubicle, fuck I am so sorry for using your desk. And for saying 'fuck' in Congress."

"It's not a church, Miss Buckenmeyer; you can use curse words here when they are appropriate." He spoke. I was going to shit myself. So this is what had happened in my cubicle. It all made sense now.

He walked toward me, busting through the invisible doors of my personal humiliation bubble, so close I could see the small silver hairs of his mustache vibrate against his smooth black skin as he exhaled.

"Oh my God, are you going to make me have sex with you now?" I whispered. I was chubby and perky and owned a beret; this is what happened to girls like me.

"Absolutely not," he answered.

"Is it because I am white?" I asked meekly.

He stared at me, neither smiling nor outraged for what felt like five solid minutes of absolute awkward silence. Then his face relaxed, and I saw the hint of a smirk spread to the corners of his mouth.

"I enjoy you, Brittany."

"I'm sorry?" I stuttered. If I threw up in that second, it would just slide down my face. I had no feeling from the eyebrows down.

"I enjoy you," he repeated, chuckling under his breath. "Tomorrow afternoon come to session with me and then we can have lunch with some of my committee colleagues."

"God, Representative, that would be amazing, thank you," I exclaimed, slowly regaining feeling in my limbs and select portions of my neck and cheeks. "I'd love to learn more about what you do to see if this whole thing is a fit for me."

"You'd make a horrible politician." He laughed. "You're a terrible liar and you almost cried twice. Grab your shoes."

He was right, I'd make a terrible politician. Running for office took a certain level of self-confidence and poise I simply didn't have. Plus once the Internet became a thing, I watched porn all the time and I'm pretty sure there's a set of naked pictures of me inside an Arby's bathroom floating around somewhere. It's crazy hard to keep that kind of thing a secret when you are running for office.

I learned to appreciate each of these internships for exactly what Jemma said they were, career blind dates. I showed up on time, learned a few lessons, got a free dinner, did an awkward bro-hug at the front door, and then never called back for a second date. And you know what, that's fine. You can't force a relationship to happen any more than you can force someone to elect you to office or be excited about hot dogs at McDonald's.

At the end of ten weeks, I lightly knocked on Jemma's door, handed her the supervisor survey the representative had kindly completed, and walked out at peace having no idea what I would be when I grew up, which ended up being pretty okay because I had plenty of things to keep me occupied, like having mental breakdowns and failing at lesbianism. We all have our journeys.

7

ADORABLY MENTAL

A MONTH BEFORE I left for Ohio State, my grandmother was diagnosed with various forms of cancer. It started in her lungs and then bounced around like a Ping-Pong ball in her body, finally culminating in the diagnosis of terminal. I can't say it was entirely surprising; she had smoked her whole life, and you couldn't sit on a couch in her living room without reaching under the cushion to find a hidden pack of Kool Menthol 100s.

Everything moved really quickly from that point. Hospice moved in, and her bedroom was transformed into a medically enabled den of comfort; oxygen machines, beeping monitors, tiny cups full of pills on her bedside table, and a large-screen television on the center of her antique dresser. None of this was meant to keep her alive, but rather present and accessible for the rest of us.

Bedridden, her small and bony frame soon took up only half of the familiar indentation worn into her mattress. I'd spend my afternoons curled up next to her under a down comforter reading aloud from gossip magazines, fashioning her silk headscarf like she was in an Erykah Badu video, and lying uncomfortably quiet beside her as she willed me random belongings from her room and shared with me all the knowledge she wouldn't get a chance to tell me later.

"All my jewelry and furs are yours," she'd whisper alongside the low hum of the oxygen from the tube in her nose. I cringed thinking of the matted rabbit fur pimp coats in her closet. It's like she had no idea that you couldn't wear that stuff in public unless you were Courtney Love.

"I like Andy, but you should really date a Filipino before you settle down; they make amazing lovers," she'd muse.

"You are going to fail at a lot of things, so when you do, do it on such a grand scale that half the room gives you a standing ovation, and the other half gives you the middle finger."

My grandmother was the most beautiful woman on earth. She had pale skin, auburn hair, and long, thin legs and fingers. She knew I didn't want to go to college. But she also knew that following Andy was my best chance of not ending up like my parents: married young, broke and struggling. My grandma and grandpa lived in a matching ranch next door, separated only by creek and some trees. When my parents were fighting or working late, I walked across the deep creek between our two houses and showed up on her front doorstep, black mud up to my knees, and spent the night.

My mom would tell me her parents were often too busy for her when she was growing up, but I found them to be a much-needed constant in my life. (I think that's a pretty normal grandparent thing, as I can now attest, my parents are way better at grandparenting than they were at parenting.) I'd nestle into the plaid couches in her living room, and she'd hum old Irish songs in the kitchen and peel the skin from apples in one long, unbroken strand. My brother always ate the apples; I always ate the skin. Then we'd watch old Judy Garland movies and drink tall glasses of orange juice like diabetes wasn't even a thing.

My grandmother had an amazing gift to make you feel like the most interesting girl in the room, and it disarmed you from feeling insecure, so you'd end up talking about yourself for hours, which felt good when you lived in a life where no one else asked. Even when she was dying, frail and thin, leaning against me as she slipped on her shoes to go to another appointment, she'd ask me what made me happy that day and kiss me on my shoulder.

"Thank you for helping me stand," she said squeezing my arm. I was thick and strong, and had spent eighteen years perfecting the art of supporting others; listening to my mom when she ached or bandaging my father when he bled. Helping her stand was the easiest thing I could do.

A week after my grandma died, I packed the back of my parents' car with suitcases of clothes, my favorite pillow, and a box of mangy fur coats. We'd both left home at the exact same time; she went to heaven, and I went to Columbus.

AGORAPHOBIA IS THE NEW VEGAN

Even though I had no idea what I was going to be when I grew up, the random English and art classes I was taking were going surprisingly well for me. Because of that, I was a fixture on the dean's list. I was also holding down a part-time job at the Gap in a nearby mall, and I was living in a two-bedroom apartment twenty minutes off campus with Andy and a pug named Lucy. We had knockoff Pottery Barn furniture, a guest room, I shopped at Whole Foods, and we had couples friends and dinner parties with wineglasses made of actual glass. We even drove nice cars, Andy the silver Nissan Altima from our first breakfast together gifted to him by his parents, and me a new VW Beetle, a car leased for me by my grandfather after the 1988 Oldsmobile I'd been driving caught fire in a mall parking lot. It was all very adult for twenty-one years old, and I loved it. I had created a simulator of the grown-up life I had always wanted. Clean, calm, comfortable, and sane.

In the summer before our fourth year of college, Andy, increasingly unhappy with his academic program at Ohio State, made the tough decision to return home and attend a local college to finish his degree. Due to the lease on our apartment and the fact that I wasn't actually failing anything, it was decided I would stay behind for the year. Andy promised to come back down to stay every weekend, but I was still very upset. We had built a life together, a couples life. We had couples friends and game nights; how could he leave that if he loved me?

"We aren't breaking up," he assured me in the parking lot of our apartment complex. "It's just one year." He kissed my tear-soaked face, pressed a gift-wrapped box into my arms, climbed into his car packed with suitcases and laundry baskets, and drove away waving.

I walked back into our now-empty apartment, Lucy snorting and wagging her curled tail expectantly at me on the couch, and felt very alone for the very first time since I started college. Sure, I was looking forward to the freedom of meeting girlfriends at dance clubs and having slumber parties with chick flicks and fizzy wine, but the truth was, I didn't know how to be alone anymore. I didn't even like ordering pizza over the phone by myself. That was an Andy job. How was I supposed to get pizza to my house now? Dependence had become addicting. I'd never had it before, relying mostly on myself for survival, but when it was suddenly stripped away it was terrifying. I had moved away from my family and gone to college and leased and apartment *with* Andy. My life had become a team sport, and I wasn't strong enough to continue doing these things by myself.

I unwrapped the small box Andy had left in my arms, and found a blank-paged spiral-bound journal with a flowing river on the front cover, which would have been a soothing if I wasn't terrified of all bodies of water. I mean seriously, you can't see how deep they are. Entire boats and sea creatures swim below you and you just are supposed to act like that's *not* happening? Inscribed on the inside cover of the journal was a note from Andy.

> *Since your current journal is almost full, I thought I'd gift you with*
> *this one to chronicle your final year of school, and your very first*
> *year living solo. I can't wait to read it, and I miss you already.*
>
> *Love Andy*

Little did he know this journal would go on to read less like an adorable coming of age story and more like *Tyler Durden, the Early Years*.

At first, living alone was exactly how I imagined it in all my Carrie Bradshaw fantasies, but it quickly became lonely and isolating. Andy's attempts to visit went from every weekend to every four to six weeks because of his class load and work commitments. It was becoming difficult to talk my friends into making the trek so far from campus to visit, and many of them didn't even have cars. Instead they'd beg me to come to weekend-long keggers in their crumbling apartments located just steps from campus. I'd want to go and have fun, but the emotions swirling in my head every minute of every day had been making me so increasingly tired, and maneuvering my car through the overcrowded streets and around burning mattresses and strangers having drunk sex next to dumpsters pushed my anxiety to its limits. I was angry, frustrated, and spent hours crying into my phone each night, begging Andy to come home, and with each excuse, no matter how valid, I evolved from being angry at being alone, to being scared to be alone.

I couldn't tell if I had just outgrown all of that youthful nonsense, or if the exhaustion, worry, and heaviness inside my brain were signs of something else, something hereditary and unavoidable and waiting inside me like a time bomb. I stopped seeing my friends, and I sent their calls straight to voice mail until one day, they simply stopped calling.

AUGUST 19, 2003

I got halfway to class today and I turned around at the stoplight. I couldn't remember if I'd triple-checked the door lock or unknowingly bumped the stove knobs with my backpack and turned on the gas. When I got into my parking lot, I also realized I may very well have left my curling iron plugged in. Thankfully I walked in to find Lucy lying in her bed unharmed and licking her crotch, and all the electronics were unplugged. But for good measure, before I leave the house each day, I've decided to stick my finger inside each socket hole and count them to double-check they are empty. There are 90 holes and I was only zapped 12 times. On the plus side, if I am ever worried I didn't unplug anything, I can just look down at my red, throbbing, electrocuted finger. Living alone is mentally exhausting; I never realized how much work Andy had to do to keep us alive each day.

Admittedly, sticking my finger into a socket sounds a little fucked-up. But the truth is pain is a tool I often use to offset my anxiety. I had my very first panic attack my junior year of high school. It came from out of nowhere. I was sitting on the couch having dinner next to my mom when suddenly it was as if I'd forgotten how to swallow. My heart sped up, my chest throbbed, and my breathing was erratic. Terrified, my mother threw me into the car and drove me to the emergency room, worried I was having a heart attack or allergic reaction. An EKG confirmed I was not, in fact, dying, but instead was having an anxiety attack. It was the most real sense of finality I'd ever experienced. Have you ever tried to put a sports bra on after getting out of the shower, and that split second where you're stuck with your arms up in the air and you think you're going to die? That is what my first panic attack felt like, and it lasted twenty minutes. I later was diagnosed with GAD (generalized anxiety disorder) and put on various types of medication. I have since spent a large portion of each day passing off my suffocating worry and doom as an adorable case of social awkwardness.

I envision my mind as a plot of grass full of sheep, surrounded by a perimeter of electric fence. If I'm not constantly vigilant and aware of my thoughts, the electric fence shuts off, the sheep jump out, and my panic gets away from me. The chance for an attack is especially bad just before bed or when I'm distracted and lost in thought in the car, causing me to slap myself in the face as hard as I can, or bite the inside of my upper arm. If I can feel the pain, then I am still alive and can begin to focus on rounding up the sheep again. See? This makes perfect sense in my head.

AUGUST 20, 2003

Executive decision . . . I am not going to class today. I tried, even drove to the damn off-campus parking lot and got on the shuttle to head to Campbell Hall, but when it stopped there, my body refused to let me get off. I rode that shuttle around the loop three fucking times. I think the other students must have thought I was in training to be a bus driver or something, which is hysterical because I can barely drive normal-sized cars. I think I need a mental health day, I can't conjugate Italian 104 verbs with a headache, anyways.

AUGUST 21, 2003

I'm having trouble getting out of my car. It takes me almost half an hour to get to the campus parking lot, but once I get there, I just

*sit in my car and listen to O.A.R. really loud and watch the fat
of my thighs spread out across the lava-hot leather seats. I don't
understand why class has to be so long. What if something happens
to Lucy or someone breaks into my apartment and then hides and
waits for me to come home? At night I hear such horrible sounds, like
someone is trying to break in or attack me. If I get out of my car and
go to class, it's like I am okay with those horrible things happening.
But, if I stay in my car, it will be fine, so I have to just stay here in my
car. Just for today.*

You are probably wondering what the hell is happening right
now. If you've never had or known someone with anxiety, most
of this looks pretty irrational. Like "Hey creep-face, stop biting
yourself and go to the classes you are paying eleventy billion dollars to attend." I'd have loved to. The issue is that as a person with
anxiety, I have the inside track on the fact that we're all doomed,
and carrying this knowledge around every second of every day is
debilitating. I can't offer you evidence or logic; I just know these
potential horrible events to be true. It's like living every day as Ben
Affleck in *Armageddon*.

AUGUST 30, 2003

*I called off work today, but Gail, my boss, told me I had already
been written off the schedule because I hadn't shown up for my shift
in over two weeks. I am somewhat concerned about how I am going
to pay rent, but more pissed at Gail. I was the only one who bought
her a baby gift last year when she had twins, and she doesn't think
that maybe she should call to check on me for two whole weeks?
What if I was dead in my apartment? What the fuck, Gail?*

I called Andy to tell him I had been fired, and he sounded
annoyed, which only made me angrier; it was as if me calling him

with my problems was bringing him down. He'd left me here and I was paying rent by myself. The two-bedroom apartment we once shared was now too big and overwhelmed my senses with noises and shadows. I didn't mention to him that I had stopped going to classes and instead spent my time sitting in the off-campus parking lot giving myself third-degree thigh burns. He promised he'd be down next month for fall break and we'd reassess the situation, but to hold tight until then. I waited until he'd hung up the phone to add, "I'll see you then, unless someone murders me first."

SEPTEMBER 6, 2003

I can't decide if my neighbor Greg is a rapist or legitimately a nice guy. I always see him outside walking his black miniature schnauzer, and today he asked me while I was letting Lucy run in the dog park next to our shared carport if I had broken up with my boyfriend. I told him no, that he'd just moved out, and then quickly realized that was not the sort of information you give to potential rapists. He offered to knock on my door each night when he was taking his dog, Bitters, out for the last time, in case I wanted to join him so I wouldn't be alone out in the dark. I said sure, because I honestly hate standing outside a dark apartment complex by myself, but I'm totally going to need to fashion a weapon to have on me just in case. Maybe I'll hide a knife in a tampon applicator, or put acetone nail polish remover in a squirt bottle like Mace? I'm still working on it. . .

Greg was not a rapist; in fact, he was perfectly lovely. Every night for a month he'd knock on my door around 8 P.M. and I'd grab Lucy and a small plastic baggie, and we'd head out for one final potty hurrah. We talked about funny television shows or how annoying the laundry room was, and he never seemed to mention the gradual change in my appearance. The way I'd meet him on the lawn wearing a dirty nightgown and Ugg boots, or when my hair had gone unwashed for five or six days. Walking Lucy outside with Greg was quickly becoming the only interaction I was having with the outside world. Everywhere else was just so loud and crowded with noise and people looking at you. One by one, my ability to handle social situations began to shut off. Nowhere felt comfortable. I wasn't going to school, I had no job, I barely showered, and then one day, when Greg knocked on my door at eight, I stopped answering.

OCTOBER 4, 2003

> *I've decided to stop going to the grocery store. I had a scary experience while loading my groceries the other day when a man sitting in the van next to me opened his door to stare at me the whole time. So, I've talked Mrs. Cho from Panda Inn into letting me order a meal over the phone and her son will walk it out to the curb where Lucy and I are parked so I don't have to get out of the car. Plus she'll throw extra napkins in the bag so I don't need to even buy toilet paper. This is my most brilliant idea ever.*

Due to my one meal of Chinese takeout a day, I was becoming vitamin deficient, my nails were breaking, I had bruises all over my legs, and I'd lost a dramatic amount of weight. I was showering only sporadically. I've watched enough *Law & Order* to know that leaving yourself vulnerable in a shower is no *bueno*. I also no longer felt safe taking Lucy outside to go to the bathroom, and spent a good portion of my day holding her over the toilet in the hopes she'd eventually just go there instead. When that failed, I hooked on her leash and led her to a black garbage bag I'd spread out on the carpet next to the front door where she'd peer up at me confused before finally giving up and shitting on the plastic. I know it seems like if you were to spend your whole entire day locked in your apartment with piles of dog shit, the days would just drag. But that wasn't the case at all. There were barely enough hours in the day for me to get through all my paranoid anxieties.

It was a few days after that when Andy and my parents showed up, courtesy of a call from my unpaid landlord, Rich, and Jemma, my concerned academic counselor, who informed them she had been unable to reach me and I had failed out of every class I had been taking that quarter. They pretended not to be horrified at the state of the once grown-up and fancy apartment now inhabited by a greasy-haired Gollum and her defecating dog. Instead Andy and my father worked quickly to pack up my belongings, and my mom bustled around the apartment with a bucket of cleaners, smiling each time she passed me sitting in shock on the couch, never hinting that I was living in squalor and that she was probably dry-heaving every time she was out of my line of vision.

In a matter of hours, the trailer behind my dad's truck had been packed with furniture, computers, and bags of clothing, and I lay against Andy in the backseat as we pulled out of the parking lot.

"Thank you for helping me stand," I whispered as he wrapped me tightly in my grandmother's mangy rabbit fur coat, and with a faint applause echoing in my brain, I weakly raised my middle finger to the failed attempt at adult life and the college degree I never earned.

8

GIRL ON GIRL INTERRUPTED

SOMETIMES, WHEN YOU have a mental breakdown in college and people are afraid to leave forks and knives around you, it takes a total environmental shift to realign your brain. At least that is what Tom my therapist told me.

I only see male therapists with mustaches. There is probably some underlying daddy issue here, but I can't be sure since I'm not a doctor. Finding shrinks with facial hair was an easier feat in the very early nineties when there was still a yuppie-mustache carryover, but by 1999, everything had gone full soul patch. This limited my choices to either very old men or hipsters. My current therapist, Tom, has a handlebar mustache and brews his own beer at home.

The first thing I did when I returned home from school was visit Tom. Tom's office was in a strip mall across from a Taco Bell, which actually worked out pretty perfectly for me, because I do my best emotionally overwhelmed eating in Taco Bell parking lots. There

were no windows in Tom's office and the walls were a deep bur-
gundy and decorated with old-timey framed photos of men playing
football in leather helmets and riding on tall bicycles with one giant
wheel and one tiny wheel. Tom sat on a brown leather chair and
offered me the long green and navy plaid couch across from him.
Instinctively, I wanted to lie down, but I always looked awkward
coming out of that position, like a turtle that had been flipped on its
back, so I just sat quietly, protectively pulling the decorative pillows
onto my lap, as fat girls are wont to do.

Once it was determined that I was in no way suicidal, which I
wasn't—in fact the majority of my day was consumed with the con-
scious effort of *not* dying—Tom decided to focus our Tuesday and
Thursday sessions on getting me on a workable medication and functioning again in adult society. He gave me menial assignments like
making vision boards or writing down my immediate daily goals
in journals. Normally, I would roll my eyes at either of those tasks,
since I've never been much of a bucket-list maker or goal setter, but
I had free time on my hands and was watching a lot of *Starting Over,*
a television show about women looking to start their lives over with
the help of inspirational life coaches and smoothies made of Oprah's
bone marrow.

I was also once again living with my parents, though my mother
had turned my old room into a temperature-controlled cockatiel
breeding room, so my "bedroom" was now a windowless section
of the garage that I shared with my pug, Lucy, who was only finally
acknowledging me again after the whole *we live among our poop* thing.

Much to my surprise, once I got home from college and showered
a few times, I woke up the next morning to find Andy lying on my
bed beside me. We had a lot of things to work on: me forgiving him
for abandoning me in Columbus to live like Edith Beale in *Grey Gar-
dens,* and him getting comfortable again with me being *me* and not

some crazy person who smelled like human waste. Neither of us was there yet, but almost.

I showed up at Tom's office Thursday holding a giant poster board with four small pictures cut out of magazines taped to it: a horse from a cigarette ad, a stack of IHOP pancakes, an old lady from a life insurance company, and a cartoon Harry Potter.

"Your vision board only has four things on it, and one of those things is Harry Potter?" he asked, furrowing his brows.

"Honestly, it's unrealistic for me to take on more than four things right now, Tom," I answered.

"Fair enough." He smiled, leaning back in his seat. "All right, tell me about the pictures."

"Well, obviously," I said, pointing at the first picture, "this is a horse. I used to like riding them, and I'd like to do that again, and also own some."

"All right, sounds therapeutic." He nodded.

"These are pancakes. They are my favorite food, and I'd like an endless supply of them."

"Right but . . ." He began to interject, but I was on a roll.

"And finally, this old lady represents my grandmother who died. I'd like to find a scientist who could bring her back or reanimate her, I haven't decided which way to go on this, but, you know, whatever they did to Shelley Long in *Hello Again*," I explained. "Oh and I'd also like to find the real Hogwarts and go there."

"This is a vision board," he explained, leaning forward. "It's supposed to be goals you want to achieve, not wishes you'd ask a genie for."

"Oh."

"Is that why you are wearing that brown robe? Is it like a Harry Potter thing?" he asked.

"Yeah, well, my mom always told me to dress for the job you

want. I guess I misunderstood this exercise," I replied, closing the robe around my body and leaning back into the couch.

"You know what? It's fine." He smiled warmly. "Forget the vision board, let's talk about what you see yourself doing in the next month or so. That way we can start giving you the tools to make some changes. Nothing big; we don't want to get over-whelmed with details and anxiety."

"Honestly," I said, exhaling, "I'd like to not live with my parents anymore, but I'm a college dropout with no job or money and everyone thinks I'm crazy."

Again it's worth noting here that I was legally an adult and hoping to legitimately find Hogwarts.

Months with Tom, and a consistent medication schedule, yielded many positive steps forward. It was decided I wouldn't go back to school, not only for my own safety, but because I really didn't want to graduate from college; everyone was just going to have to learn to accept that about me. (Also, if someone could please explain that to the collections lady for my student loans, that'd be great.) We worked on techniques to get my panic attacks under control, and Tom listened to each of my irrational fears with a calm demeanor and an accepting nod.

My time in Columbus was the perfect storm of mental events. I had gone from being a child caretaker of my parents to putting my self-reliance on cruise control with Andy, who was awesome at managing my security and life decisions. When Andy left and that was suddenly gone, I panicked and was unable to refocus and take care of myself. None of it was healthy, but all of it was fixable. I just needed to learn how to be a grown-up.

I could watch the change of seasons unfold by the change of Tom's mustache, and by spring, when his handlebar had morphed into a more generic Borat, I told Tom that I'd applied to work at an all-girls summer camp based on my love of the movies *Meat-*

balls and *Wet Hot American Summer.* I then asked him if it was okay to make all my future life decisions based on movies I enjoyed. I honestly don't remember his answer. Something like, "I like Paul Rudd. Is nice."

CAMP LESBIAN

I got a job working at an all-girls summer camp located in northwest Ohio, along the Maumee River. During the summer it functioned as a sleepaway camp and in the off season could be rented out by school groups. Having spent many summers there myself as a kid, being back at camp as an adult was a surreal experience. Tom also felt this was a great way for me to practice being a human in society again within a controlled environment; plus it meant I was no longer living with my parents. I had responsibilities, coworkers, social interaction, and duties that required problem-solving, but no Internet or germ-free shower facilities. Camp functioned as a rudimentary microsociety within a society, with its own schedules and dramas unrelated to anything going on in the outside world. It was like being on *Survivor* but with running water and decent food.

At orientation, I sat on a wooden log next to a twenty-something girl with shoulder-length curly hair and knee-high compression socks, the same socks you'd see on elderly women seated in pharmacies waiting for their prescriptions. Of the maybe forty of us counselors, ranging in age from eighteen to twenty-eight, only four were boys, and three of them were gay. We were dressed the same in long khaki shorts, tennis shoes and deep purple uniform shirts with "Camp" embossed across the front. It was the nicest and cleanest any of us would look all summer. As we sat around the unlit campfire that afternoon, a series of directors and executive staff welcomed us to camp, stressed our roles as mentors to the incoming kids, and went over various camp lifesaving scenarios; choking, drowning, sunburn, EpiPens, bears, tornados. Two things they didn't prepare us for? Raging UTIs and what to do when you find your tween campers in a tent huffing bug spray.

We then filled out legal releases and emergency medical forms, and picked a camp nickname the campers would use when addressing us. I am not 100 percent sure why this was a thing, but it's either to make the whole experience that much more magical for the kids, or to dehumanize us to the point that the camp director didn't feel bad asking us to scrub human shit from the beds and nightgowns of crying girls. We were also able to select our top program choices. My camp name was Blue (like the old guy from *Old School,* duh) and I wanted to work with the six-to-eight-year-olds because small children are adorable and teenagers frighten me. I was so excited; I was in the woods being paid to play with children all day. How did I ever get so lucky?

One week into camp, I sat across the table in the dining hall at lunch, beads of sweat rolling down my neck and onto the butt-shaped cleavage created by my sports bra, and watched a seven-year-old girl drink a soup bowl of ranch dressing the way you finish off the last of your milk in cereal. Turns out, I am not built for working with small kids after all. Between the homesickness and the bedwetting and the shoe tying and the fact kids are sometimes the most disgusting humans on earth, my ovaries separated themselves and fell out of my vagina. A week later I was transferred to the horse barn.

The days at the barn were long, smelly, and excruciatingly hot, but they were quiet and drama-free, which I loved. It was also an excuse to get out of the standard counselor uniform of shorts and a loose T-shirt, as the barn required long pants and boots. It was miserable in the afternoon sun, but as any girl with a decent amount of thigh rub can attest, jeans in the summer was a welcome break from picking ridden-up shorts out of your crotch.

I cleaned stalls, organized tack, fed, groomed, and spent hours shoving spazzy girls on and off western saddles. I related to the fifteen horses in our care. They were brought into camps for small children because they were old, tired, and had generally stopped giving a fuck. I felt the same way most days. I worked side by side with another counselor named Sprinkle, who shared an equal amount of disdain for loud children and as an act of protest to the war in Iraq, refused to say the pledge of allegiance during the flag raising each morning. She was easily one of my favorite people at camp. Second only to Mary, the cook in the kitchen who gave me extra tater tots.

Sprinkle was tiny, maybe five feet tall, with long black hair, freckles, and a uniform of skinny jeans and tall yellow mud boots. We were roommates in a platform tent, and at night we'd lie in bed and share stories about our lives and the boyfriends we were missing. Her boyfriend Jakob was studying photography and was making a coffee-table book out of photos taken in filthy gas station bathrooms. Andy and I were keeping our recovering relationship open and relaxed while I was at camp and he was finishing up his degree in computer engineering.

What the weeklong sessions lacked in mental stimulation, the weekends made up for in absolute depravity. By the time the last camper had been loaded into their parents' minivan to head home Friday afternoon, my fellow counselors and I were already two beer bongs in. In my entire life, I had never witnessed such drunken degeneracy, and we were in charge of your children. Cases of beer and bags of pot, we stumbled around intoxicated like every weekend was Fleet Week. After hours of doing shots, playing beer pong, and singing off-tune Oasis songs around the fire, we'd stumble back to our tents to rest before doing it all again the next day. I was living the carefree young adult life I missed out on in high school because nobody liked me and in college when I passed on parties to see foreign films with my boyfriend. I was sewing my fat-girl oats. It was bliss.

"Hey," Sprinkle whispered.

"Hey," I whispered back, my eyes heavy with exhaustion and cheap beer.

"If I don't have sex soon my vagina is going to fall off."

"I know, right?" I answered. "I leaned into a canter today for twenty solid minutes."

"We should just have sex with each other and get it over with," she sighed.

"Absolutely," I said with a laugh, falling back into my sleeping bag.

She climbed out of bed and padded over to my cot; leaning over my face she lightly kissed me on the lips. She smelled like alcohol and vanilla shampoo and it was intoxicating. She kissed me again slower and slipped her tongue into my mouth.

I pulled my head back confused. "It's just that, I've never been a lesbian before outside of watching *The L Word?*"

"My sister is a gay," Sprinkle explained. "She said it was way easier than sex with guys. We already know how all the parts work."

I sat up in my cot and slowly removed my shirt, revealing the double sports bras I'd been wearing so my boobs didn't bounce so much during trail rides. We both stood up to take off our jeans and looked each other over. Unlike with boys, I wasn't self-conscious or ashamed of my body in front of Sprinkle. Camp wasn't full of supermodels or celebrities; it was full of nature lovers and social rejects, all desperate to escape the real world for a while. Sprinkle was athletic with a short torso and abs. I was tall with a roll of belly fat sitting above my underwear. To the outsider, we might look ridiculous, but between the beer and the mutual level of unshaved leg and armpit hair, we called it a draw.

I reached my hand out to touch her breasts, but it was as if I had transformed into a thirteen-year-old boy fumbling around boobies with the romance of a breast self-exam.

"I'm sorry," I explained. "I don't know what to do with my hands."

"It's fine," she assured me quickly. "Let's just get to the climax stuff so we can go to bed."

"Great idea," I answered, totally unconvincing to even myself.

"Have you ever been eaten out?" she asked, her breath hitching in her throat.

"I have, listen, is that the plan here, because I've been riding horses all day and—"

"Good point," she interrupted. "Let's go freshen up with the hose outside." She grabbed my hand and dragged me pantsless down the platform steps to the rusty faucet outside our tent. Taking turns, we washed our bodies with the freezing water and between blacked-out moments of drunken confusion, I found myself positioned between her naked open legs on the floor of our tent. I lay on my stomach, propping myself up with my elbows. This was an important life moment. This was no longer going to be, *Oh sure, I've kissed girls in bars because I'm flirty and adorable;* this was going to be, *Oh yeah, I had my mouth on an actual vagina.* I leaned forward, holding my breath.

"Yeah, I can't do this." I exhaled. "It looks funny."

"Wait, funny like something's wrong?" Sprinkle sat up alarmed.

"No!" I assured her. "I just never saw it from this angle before, and I can't touch it with my mouth. I mean, I barely eat scallops without gagging, and this definitely looks like it has the same feeling as a scallop."

"My vagina looks like a scallop?" she asked sadly.

"It's a texture thing. I probably have a scallop vagina, too," I assured her. "I'm sorry, I'm a terrible lesbian."

"It's fine." She sighed. "I'm going to go see if Scooter and Tank are done jerking each other off in the boys' restroom. Maybe one of them can play it straight for a couple of minutes."

Failing at female oral sex was yet another freeing realization I had that summer. Unlike the real world, where my failures left me weak and powerless on the floor of a filthy apartment, the fumbles and missteps I made at camp opened me up to amazing opportunities. As long as no kids died and my bunkmate still talked to me the morning after I called her vagina a mollusk, I was fine. Incidentally, Sprinkle and I remain friends to this day, and I was a bridesmaid in her wedding. I assume her husband is way better at oral sex than I was. The point of this all is that it taught me that when I fucked up, I could get back up and I could either try again or face the consequences, which were completely manageable. I left at the end of the summer with photos I can never show my children and a backpack full of camp lessons that have gone on to be surprisingly applicable to this very day:

1. Bug Juice has zero nutritional value and makes for a horrible mixer for alcohol.
2. You are never too old for friendship bracelets.
3. If you sleep in your bathing suit, you will get a yeast infection.
4. Your pee is way less hot and gross than other people's pee, especially when it's on the bedding you're stripping from the bunk of a sobbing seven-year-old.
5. Camp gay is like prison gay. What happens in the woods stays in the woods.
6. Counselors are the craziest and biggest drunks you will ever meet in your whole entire life.
7. I am never ever sending my kids to camp.

A week after camp ended, I returned to Tom's office for my weekly therapy appointment with tan skin and callouses on my hands, carrying a poster board with pictures of wedding dresses and Ron Weasley.

"Welcome back." Tom smiled, leaning back into his leather chair and stroking the goatee he'd grown in my absence. "Now, tell me about the pictures."

9

GOING TO THE CHAPEL

ANDY ASKED ME to marry him on a freezing November night, in a crumbling stone chapel filled with candles, in the middle of a goddamn cemetery. No YouTube videos or flash mobs, just me, him, a groundskeeper named Gary, and a bunch of corpses. That's just how every little girl envisions it, right? I obviously said yes, because I've seen how the "Thriller" video ends, I'm not a fast runner, and being chased by the undead wouldn't pan out well for me.

"I can't believe you asked me to marry you in a cemetery," I said as his shaky hands slipped the beautiful pavé diamond ring on my finger.

"You said it was beautiful here." He looked up confused.

"It is beautiful here," I assured him. "On a Tuesday afternoon, when I'm bringing flowers to my grandma's grave and other people with pulses are here."

I can think of no greater reflection of our relationship than being proposed to in a cemetery. It's weird, off-putting, defies logic, and gets funnier every time we retell the story. I had been waiting for that moment for eight years. We'd survived high school, college, some mental breakdowns, and a bout of lesbianism of which Andy asks me to recount with the same magical glint in his eye as children gathering around to hear "The Night Before Christmas."

What I didn't expect was that the moment in the cemetery when he slipped that ring on my finger was the moment the wedding process would peak.

THE ENGAGEMENT

Point blank, I did not want a large wedding. My parents couldn't afford it and I'd parlayed my limited event-planning experience from college into working as the wedding coordinator at the Toledo Country Club. This job gave me a front-row seat to absolutely every horrible aspect of weddings . . . the largest being the bride. In my opinion, brides are horrible, horrible people. They are erratic, indecisive, and will come down on you with the wrath of God should you cross them. And they don't mean it; outside of getting married, brides are typically normal and even enjoyable humans to be around. It's just that something inside them takes over and they turn into domestic terrorists.

I once watched a Discovery documentary about these ants in South Carolina that ate a fungus that essentially killed them and then went on to control their dead bodies like reanimated zombies. I find that to be a similar process to brides planning their weddings, and I wanted to avoid that. My plan was to elope in Vegas with some close friends and a corny Elvis.

Andy wanted a large wedding, or at least he claimed his parents did. I don't know that they wanted a large wedding so much as *no* wedding. After he proposed in the cemetery, Andy and I had dinner in a dimly lit Lebanese restaurant in South Toledo called Byblos. It was an old-school sort of place that was almost always empty save for quiet couples sitting on the same side of a four-person booth or expensively dressed mobsters passing envelopes of money beneath white silk napkins. They also have the best lamb in town.

Andy sat across from me at a small round table dressed with billowing white silk linens, squeezed my newly baubled hand, smiled, and then quietly asked me to not tell anyone we were engaged.

"Why wouldn't I tell anyone?" I asked, confused.

"Isn't it more fun when it's a secret only you and I know?" he pushed.

"No, it feels like you're embarrassed or afraid to tell people you asked me to marry you," I countered. The magic of our evening dimmed slightly as I considered his request and its contribution to my already prominent insecurities. This was a happy moment for me, and I wanted people to be excited for and with us. That is what weddings were, public declarations of love. If it was a secret, people would get married in their homes on a Tuesday through the mail with the same pomp and circumstance as absentee voting.

"Let's just enjoy the weekend, okay?" he pleaded. "We can tell people next week, but right now, it's just ours."

I conceded to secrecy for the weekend, but that Monday we sat in his parents' kitchen, our arms resting on the shiny white marble as his mother leaned against the counter flipping through the Sunday paper.

"We have news," Andy started by saying. His voice was weaker than normal.

His mom looked up and smiled, thoughtlessly flipping the pages as if she were still reading.

"I proposed and we're getting married," he announced with the same enthusiasm he'd showed that morning when he asked me to smell the milk to see if it was still good.

"Are you serious?" she asked, her eyes darting side to side

between us before finally tearing up. They weren't happy tears, as evidenced by the way she shook her head no and clawed at her neck as if someone had struck her with a poisonous dart and she wasn't sure from which direction it had come.

"We're really excited," I said assertively, holding my hand with the ring up and waving my fingers, hoping to match the happiness that moments like these have on mall jewelry store commercials.

An eerie smile spread across his mother's face as she nodded politely and backed out of the room, leaving us once again alone. Andy looked at me and smiled weakly. He had known all along that this would happen, and perhaps I did, too. Yes, I wanted to tell his parents we were engaged because it's exciting and magical, but part of me also wanted them to have absolutely no choice but to accept me, legally.

The summer after our senior year of high school, Andy's mother took him and me on a weekend vacation to Virginia Beach, and as I was changing in the hotel room she walked in and saw the large monarch butterfly I'd had tattooed on my left hip. I had gotten that tattoo on my fifteenth birthday from a friend's dad without my parent's permission. Up until that moment, I had successfully hidden it from both of our parents. She frowned, inquired if it was real, and then walked out. I'd felt so ashamed and embarrassed that when I got home, I showed my parents the poorly drawn tattoo and begged them to help me pay to get it removed.

That December, while most college freshmen were at home enjoying their first school break, the plastic surgeon who'd handled many of my great-uncle Frank's facelifts was carefully cutting the tattoo from my stomach and stitching the large butterfly-shaped hole back together. I told everyone back at campus my dad made me remove it, and they nodded their heads in agreement: "Fathers are the worst." But the reality was, I'd done it for Andy's mother. I never wanted her to look at me that way again.

My mom had a saying: "Never date a man who drives a van." Also, that you don't marry a person, you marry his whole family. Andy had long since been accepted into mine, present at every family holiday gathering and smiling in every family photo. I sat on the stool in his parents' kitchen and put my hand on the scar of my left hip. If going under the knife wasn't enough to win her heart, maybe a family wedding would. We were having a big wedding.

JUST SAY YES TO EVERYTHING I SAY, OKAY?

Planning a wedding should be easy. I mean, I did it for a living; weddings were my jam. Right off the bat, I made a few nonnegotiable demands. I wanted to get married in the winter, in a church, and I wanted to look like Grace Kelly. I mean, if we were going to do this, we were going to do it big.

All of this would have been infinitely easier and cheaper had I not foolishly joined an online wedding forum of brides-to-be, you know, to get tips. The plan was to keep things simple and affordable since we were paying for this ourselves. I wasn't going to fall into the pricey trap I've seen so many brides in my office tumble down, demanding monogrammed chair covers and color-specific candy buffets. No, no, no, that wasn't us at all.

But one evening Andy walked into the bedroom to find me pacing the floor, holding my laptop, piles of bridal magazines at my feet.

"Did you know that the napkin fold you have at your wedding is a direct reflection of your life together as a couple?" I asked, my right eye twitching slightly.

"Okay?" he agreed nervously.

"So what fold are we?" I pressed. "Are we a pyramid fold or a French fold? And don't say a fanfold because everyone agrees fanfolds end in divorce."

It was like some sort of mob mentality had taken over. I was no longer making decisions on my own; I was posting them to the forum to be voted up or down by legions of anonymous women who shared my distaste for Jordan almonds and cash bars.

"Babe, do you want to start looking at DJs?" Andy asked over dinner.

"The girls and I agree that DJs are for bat mitzvahs and raves; we should really be interviewing bands," I answered matter-of-factly.

When it came time to book the ceremony location, a whole new persona had taken over: I was suddenly the most religious person in the world. I hadn't actually set foot into a church in years, yet the moment the white gold encircled my ring finger, it was like I was the pope.

We met with the priest of my home parish in his small residence next to the church. He was tall, dressed in simple jeans and a white button-down shirt, and resembled an old Andy Griffith. We discussed our goals for the wedding and talked a bit about our relationship. He offered us glasses of whiskey and spent an hour explaining the importance of a strong Catholic foundation for marriage. By the second glass he began to repeat himself, and I was growing impatient.

"If I give you a list of facts about our lives, will you pretend to know us, make inside jokes during the ceremony, and act like we're really good friends, like on *The Sopranos* or something?" I asked.

"That's an odd request." He suddenly sobered and squinted at me in confusion.

"I'll make an additional donation?" I offered.

"Well, amen." He conceded.

I don't know who I was trying to impress, since I've never looked at someone who was on a first-name basis with their priest and thought, *Man, how cool is that motherfucker right there?* But I needed this experience to happen. I had no idea who I was anymore.

THE DRESS

If you are over a size 10, wedding dress shopping can be a really awful experience. Never mind that formal wear in general has a standard of sizing equivalent to a small Asian girl; the sample dresses kept by most bridal salons do not go above a size 8.

I had asked Andy's mother to join us as we shopped for dresses. Because she has only two boys, I assumed this was a special experience she'd otherwise miss out on. I immediately regretted this decision when I came out of the fitting room in a gown attached to my size-18 body with a series of industrial-strength chip clips.

"The front is pretty," she said, touching her fingertips to her chin in thought. "It's just hard to tell what the back will look like since it won't close."

My mom smiled at me warmly as she and the fitting room attendant pulled at the back of the white satin dress.

"You can order this dress in any size," the attendant assured me, winking.

I tried on three more dresses, one of them so slim I was unable to put it on, and instead came out of the dressing room with it attached to the front of my body with a giant human hair tie, before finally falling in love with a strapless champagne-colored lace ball gown with a small satin bow around the waist. It looked as if it had fallen out of an old movie, and I cried when I saw my reflection standing up on that carpeted pedestal. The attendant smiled in agreement and began jotting down my measurements on her clipboard, and I twirled around as the fabric swung around me, picturing myself wearing it on the big day, or absolutely any other scenario that had me sashaying around in a dress that zipped, and not one spread open in the back displaying my flimsy strapless bra and mounds of back fat. It would take ten to twelve weeks for that experience, but the thin brides got to have it right away.

THE INVITATIONS

Despite my intense micromanaging of the event so far, I actually had very few concerns about what the wedding invitations looked like. I tried to care, I even looked at a few catalogs, but as long as they were cute, went out on time, and were not whatever size the U.S. Postal Service charges a hundred dollars each to mail, I was cool with them. What pissed me off about the invitations was that I had to buy them . . . twice.

It snowed early that year. We usually don't see snow in Ohio until right around Christmas, but that year it came a whole month ahead of schedule and I was absolutely giddy about it. I am a cold-weather girl, and prefer jeans and sweaters to sticky skin and shorts.

I curled up at the dining room table with a cup of tea and a Dean Martin Christmas CD in the player and began to address the mountain of wedding invitations. I had taken an introductory cal-ligraphy class at my library, and my handwriting sat somewhere between bubbly high school girl and Shakespeare.

Andy was out at a friend's bachelor party for the evening, so the knock at the door before 10 P.M. startled me. I opened the front door of the split-level home we were renting in town to find Andy laughing and tipsy against his friend Mark.

"What happened?" I asked, helping Andy through the door and up the steps to our living room.

"Your boy can't hold his liquor," Mark said with a laugh. He was right; Andy rarely drank. I selfishly enjoyed that aspect of him since it meant I'd always have a designated driver.

Mark helped me get Andy situated on the couch and pulled off his shoes before heading back out to the party.

"Can I bring you anything?" I asked Andy. He looked uncharacteristically pitiful.

"C'mere," he slurred. "I hafta tell you something."

"Baby, I'm trying to get these invitations addressed and in the mail by morning."

"No, really. C'mere." He looked suddenly serious, sitting up and putting his head in his hands.

"What's wrong?" I sat down beside him and put my hand against his back. I could feel his breath speed up a little and soon realized he was crying. "Andy, you're scaring me, what happened?"

He looked at me suddenly, his eyes red and teary. "I kissed someone."

I'm not sure what I had expected to hear. Maybe that he'd lost too much money gambling at the casino where they'd eaten dinner or that they'd hit someone with their car on the way home and didn't call the police. I literally expected any form of murder before I expected to hear that he'd kissed someone else.

"I'm so sorry," he sobbed, searching my face for reaction.

I closed my eyes, bile churning in my stomach. I didn't want to scream or cry, I wanted to throw up. I breathed in deeper as the nausea worsened.

"Is she thinner than me?" I asked finally.

Because it had to be that, right? I didn't even see girls as prettier than me anymore, only thinner, and therefore better across the board. My biggest fear, that I would wake up and everyone would say, *Just kidding, this has been one giant elaborate joke, no one wants to marry you after all*, was coming true.

"It doesn't matter," he said.

Wrong answer. To me, to a girl who has always been fat and always felt less-than, it does matter. At least at the time it did.

"I have to leave," I said suddenly. I stood up and walked into the kitchen looking for car keys. Andy bounded off the couch following me, frantic and scared.

"Where are you going?" he asked, his eyes wide and fearful.

"I have to leave. I'm going to be sick."

With one swoop of my arm, I gathered the invitations into the giant box on the chair, opened the second-story kitchen window, and tossed them out into the falling snow.

"Stop," he pleaded, my movements almost robotic as I picked up Lucy with my free arm and my purse and keys in the other.

I walked to the garage and got into the black Ford Explorer I'd bought after camp because it felt like more of a family car and put it into reverse, but before I could back out, Andy dove behind the car and lay down on the ground behind my tires.

"What are you doing?!" I screamed. "I could kill you! Get up!"

"Not until you talk to me!" he shouted back.

I sat silent in the car for ten minutes as Andy lay on the asphalt covered in snow. Lucy looked at me, frankly embarrassed for the both of us. I sighed heavily and got out of the car. Seeing the door open, Andy leapt to his feet, meeting me at the driver's door shivering and pale.

"She kissed me," he explained. "She was a friend of Mike's and she kissed me and I didn't stop her fast enough."

I winced.

"I can't tell you if she was thinner because I don't see women anymore," he continued. "I only see you, and everyone else is just noise. Please. Don't leave me."

I didn't want to leave. I didn't even want to pretend I wanted to leave.

"I threw the invitations out the window," I said finally.

"I know, I saw." He smiled cautiously. "You are crazy and I love that about you."

I laughed and wiped my running nose with the cuff of my sweatshirt and then wrapped my arms around my body.

"Our wedding is in a month and we have no invitations?"

"So we'll make them," he said, suddenly hit once again with drunken enthusiasm.

And make them we did.

THE PARENTS OF THE BRIDE

"Your dad wants to know if he has to wear the tuxedo the whole time," my mom said into the phone.

I pulled the receiver from my ear and silently mimed smashing it onto the counter in front of me.

"Yes, he has to wear the tux the whole time," I sighed.

"And the shoes?" she asked again.

"Yes," I answered calmly.

"Keith! She said you have to wear the tux and the shoes the whole time!" she yelled into the distance behind her.

"That's fine," she said, returning to our phone call. "He'll wear the shoes around the house to break them in, but he doesn't like the tuxedo pants. He says they are hard to squat in."

I THEE WED

I walked down the aisle to "Ave Maria" at six o'clock on a cold December evening, followed by an obnoxious reception featuring Rat Pack impersonators, poker tables, and food catered by our favorite Chinese takeout spot. Andy's mother wore white, the priest forgot my name, and my dad took his shoes off. It was truly a night to remember.

"I am not even sure we are legally married," Andy said, falling backward onto the mattress sitting on the floor of our bedroom.

"What are you talking about, of course we're married," I assured him sleepily, my muscles sore from dancing and feasting on Chinese food.

"You said 'I Brittany Take You Drew,'" he shot back.

"I told you I wanted you to change your name to the Drew part of Andrew, and I thought this would be the final push you needed."

"But my license says Andy. I think you just lied in front of God."

"Well if God is checking licenses to get into heaven, I'm fucked because I lied about my weight on there, too." I laughed.

"You can get it corrected when you go to the DMV to change your name to Mrs. Gibbons," he added. "Mrs. Gibbons, one hundred and ten pounds."

I sighed. "This is why I married you. You think I weigh a hundred and ten pounds."

10

THE LIFE AND DEATH OF PROCREATION AND ALL THE GROSS SHIT IN BETWEEN

THEY SAY THE ultimate act of love is having a baby. I say the ultimate act of love is deciding to not have babies, so much so that you are willing to have your ball sack cut open to make that happen. This is how I found myself on the other side of the recovery room staring at my husband's swollen and hairless testicles. Love had brought us here.

Three years earlier, love had looked much different. I remember standing in the living room of our rented yellow split-level house, holding the spoon I'd been using to stir shrimp scampi on the stovetop when I'd heard the news anchor make the announcement. Andy walked through the front door from work moments later and found me still standing stone-faced staring at the television.

"What's wrong?" he asked, panic spreading across his face.

"Britney Spears is pregnant," I answered, turning to him with tears in my eyes.

It was just like people in generations before me who would always remember where they were when John Kennedy was shot. I now know how ridiculous it is that I'd hung my emotional happiness on a pop star, aside from the fact that we are the same age and have the same name, hers, of course, spelled incorrectly. Andy and I had been trying to have a baby for six months, and while that isn't a long time in fertility terms, it felt like forever when it had been browbeaten into us in high school that if you let a penis hang out in your vagina, or even get in questionable hot tubs, you will get pregnant. One time in high school I had accidental anal sex with a wrestler named Kyle who had one testicle, and even though it wasn't vaginal sex, I was so freaked out about it, my body made my period be one week late. I had spent every night in my room before my period came rehearsing how I was going to tell my parents I was pregnant and having a baby with a high school wrestler I'd had butt sex with. So wrapping my head around the fact that it was taking a long time to get pregnant through my vagina with my husband was difficult, and I found the whole high school sex education message to be very misleading. I almost wish that women's bodies prevented them from getting pregnant until they reached a certain age, or voted in one nonpresidential election, or knew how to change a flat tire on a busy highway.

As a twenty-four-year-old not-pregnant person, I found that every baby announcement and new episode of *Teen Mom* began to sting. I was perfectly healthy and a voluptuous size 18. My obstetrician, the aging Dr. Sim, who years before had once peeled Scotch tape from my vagina, was now thoughtfully checking over my chart each visit, encouraging me to keep trying, and while never outright asking me to lose weight, he ended every visit with a smile and a gentle pat to my belly, saying "Get healthy in here, it's better for the baby."

I'd been living on a diet of salmon and apples because I read online they made for a hospitable cervix and increased blood flow to my reproductive organs. Sex had become less about intimacy and more of a game of how many things I could cram under my butt after my husband came inside me. Pillows, piles of clothes, unassembled boxes of IKEA furniture, the higher I could get my ass in the air, the more likely gravity would help the sperm do their jobs. I'd sit there elevated for hours, one time watching the entirety of *Pearl Harbor,* which as we all know is about three hundred hours too long. But it worked; it was after that showing that I stood up not only with a massive UTI but also impregnated with the help of Ben Affleck, Jon Voight, Cuba Gooding Jr., and Andy Gibbons.

As in many of our life decisions, Andy and I were relatively early in the game compared to our peers. We were the first to get married and the first to move into a house, and now we were the first to get pregnant. When I told my friend Lindsey over lunch, she grabbed my hand wide-eyed and said, "Oh shit, what are you going to do?"

I was going to have a baby, Lindsey, on *purpose.*

WELL, THIS IS SUCKIER THAN I THOUGHT IT WOULD BE

At eight weeks Andy and I walked eagerly into our very first prenatal appointment. It's all very standard and noneventful. I met with the nurse as she rattled off a million medieval diseases that I may have possibly had, and I said no to all of them except for water elf disease; she gave me a captain's log worth of blood work scripts, and sent me on my way with a huge bag full of free products, which is the main reason why I got knocked up in the first place. I am a swag whore. But, despite the endless influx of free changing pads and a full-color Fetus of the Month calendars, pregnancy wasn't the rainbows and bubble-gum that *Rosemary's Baby* had painted it to be.

I've assembled a list of my top fat-girl pregnancy pros and cons.

This list is actually really similar to a normal pregnancy pros and cons list, because even though we're curvy, we're still basically human and our reproductive organs are in the same general area, right under the rib cage, above them empty cans of Red Bull.

Con: The high-risk pregnancy.

I hate to come right out of the gate with a negative, but this is a real slap to the newly pregnant glow of many overweight expecting women. Because of my size, around 190 pounds when I got pregnant I was sent to the maternal fetal medicine department of my local hospital to see a high-risk neonatologist. I sat in the waiting room among anxious women there for very different reasons, some for genetic disorders, others for congenital anomalies. I was there because of my pants size. I felt embarrassed but also vastly insignificant. Here were families facing very scary statistics and outcomes, and I was waddling in to take up an entire appointment to reinforce what was already blatantly obvious: my fat body was growing a baby. The only thing I was at a high risk of was consuming all the cupcakes.

Pro: The dreams.

I don't know what happens in pregnancy exactly; perhaps it's the moment in life when the layer between real life and *The Matrix* is the thinnest, but holy hell, I think I just climaxed. The majority of my dreams during pregnancy were sexual and very realistic. Every time I closed my eyes it was like the orgy scene of *Eyes Wide Shut*. The feelings and images became so blurred against reality, I began to forget if it was just a dream or I'd actually just had sex. Andy would wake me up expectantly each morning, only to find me already blissfully postcoital and uninterested.

"Aren't you supposed to be really into sex while pregnant?" he'd ask, confused at my indifferent annoyance.

"I am," I assured him. "I've just done it twice and I'm exhausted."

Con: The Glucose Tolerance Test.

In an effort to detect and curb the instance of gestational diabetes in pregnant women, we are herded into laboratories around the twenty-four-week mark to drink a bottle of sugar solution and have our blood checked an hour later to ensure our glucose levels are within normal range. There isn't anything particularly horrible about this whole thing except that downing goblets of flat Fanta on an empty stomach is a little bit vomit inducing. Even though I passed my one-hour test with flying colors, I was still made to take the three-hour test, which included multiple blood draws over the course of two additional hours, as a precaution due to my weight and fearmongering words like *Obesity! Preeclampsia! Sixteen-pound baby on the cover of* US Weekly!

Con: The stomach.

When you are overweight, it takes just a little bit longer for the baby bump to show up. For a while you just walk around looking like you live on an endless supply of Chinese takeout and beer, until one day you finally pop, thus confirming the baby you swear to every stranger giving you the side-eye in the grocery store you're totally having. It took me twenty-two weeks to finally show during my first pregnancy; dogs are only pregnant for nine weeks. It took me over two entire dog pregnancies to look human pregnant.

Pro: The stomach, seriously.

Okay, so when I finally did look pregnant, I fell in love with my body. It was as if all my curves had been legitimized, and my abs had never been so rock hard. Sure, you could do an endless supply of core work and a diet of lean proteins, or you could just fill your stomach with babies. I don't have to tell you which option sounds more logical; it's obviously baby abs.

Con: The weirdos.

Pregnancy elicits two weird responses from bystanders. First, everyone wants to talk to you about their birth stories. I barely look my mail lady in the eye, but I do know that her second son was breech and covered in baby poop when he came out. I also know that Andy's great aunt tore from tit to taint giving birth to his uncle. It's like the way old people like to talk to you about the war; these women went through vagina hell, and you're obligated to sit and listen to it out of respect and patriotism.

And if that isn't awkward enough, they want to touch your stomach in a very stranger-danger fashion. Bonus points if they hum while they do it. To combat this, I gently place one finger, the one that smelled like the burrito I just ate, across their lips shushing them, and then place my free hand softly across their genitals, almost cupping them, and then sigh dreamily. Creepiness doesn't have to be a one-player game.

Con: The big . . . ger boobs.

Big boobs sounds like a pro, and in truth, it's nice to have perky boobs every now and then. But at some point they just get so engorged they are downright suffocating. It's like living your whole life with the neck pillow people take on airplanes sitting backward across your face.

Pro: The parking spaces.

If this decade has brought us anything, its new-age narcissism, and I love it. Overpriced organic supermarkets that sell us the food people in third-world countries involuntarily eat to survive, forward-facing cameras on our cell phones, and pregnancy parking spots. Finally, someone realized that being pregnant puts us in the same category as the handicapped. If this isn't happening where you live yet, write your congressman. It's hard unwedging myself from behind the steering wheel. It's hard walking more than three yards without urine slipping out. Now if only they could add a few more close spots for hangovers, I might actually venture into public more, thus spending more money, and boom, that's how you stimulate a dragging economy, Mr. President.

Con: The hypochondria.

When I was about fourteen weeks along, I accidentally shocked myself on an exposed area of the cord on my curling iron. Naturally, I assumed I had just electrocuted and cooked my baby. Hysterical, I called my OB, who calmly tried to assure me that the baby was probably fine, to which my response was "whatever." I then had Andy drive me to the ER to explain to them what I had done and to check and see if the baby had been fried by my curling iron. The entire car ride there I keep asking Andy if he'd smelled cooked meat and if he'd still love me if I'd killed out baby over vanity. It turns out I'm a psycho and amniotic fluid isn't even a conductor. Seriously, you could stand in a puddle holding an umbrella and get struck by lightning and your baby probably wouldn't cook like a turkey. But basic logic and rationale didn't matter to me in my pregnant state. Keeping me alive was hard enough. Keeping another person alive inside my body was a nightmare. But not as much of a nightmare as cholera, which I was totally convinced I had.

Con. The fashion.

Plus-size maternity is barely a thing. Plus-size people sometimes wearing maternity clothes is a thing, but actual clothes developed for pregnant plus-size people is exceedingly hard to come by.

"When I was pregnant, I just wore my husband's sweats and T-shirts around. I didn't care that people thought I was sloppy," my friend Melissa once stated matter-of-factly.

That's adorable, Melissa. But I don't even fit into my husband's clothing when I'm not pregnant. In fact, if my house was on fire, and we had to jump out of the window with only what we could safely grab, and I accidentally grabbed my husband's jeans? I would have no pants. I'd be standing next to a fire truck watching my house burn down with no pants on unless a really giant fireman, like the out-of-shape one they let roll up the hose and drive the truck, let me wear his fireman outfit.

I don't know if they assume plus-size people don't get pregnant because *eww,* or if they just assume we'd be fine buying larger sizes of our already disproportioned clothes. Either way, dressing myself in the height of my maternity meant embracing options that dated me back to Kid N' Play times. Which is why I wore giant men's overalls with one strap hooked to my baby shower.

Con: The diet.

The average woman is told she can gain around 20–25 pounds during the course of her pregnancy. I was told I could gain 10 pounds. So, naturally, I gained 60 pounds. Restricting my cravings during my pregnancy made be very bitter, and as a result, I revenge-ate quite a bit. This happens to me in my nonpregnant life as well, and is a huge reason dieting doesn't work for me; it makes me resentful. I get angry at the people who don't diet. I get angry that I can't live like they do. I mourn, in a very real way, a life I will never have. And during my pregnancy I was so envious and angry at the depictions of pregnant women enjoying their indulgences and sending their spouses out for ice cream at 2 A.M. that the thought of not being able to do that took a large part of the experience of a normal pregnancy away from me. I didn't expect my pregnancy to be like a movie cliché, but I do expect to be able to have steak fajitas and sauerkraut when I'm craving them. To combat the weight gain anxiety, I just began standing on the OB's scale backward. If I don't see it, it's not really happening, and I can just gauge my failure based on the level of sighing from my nurse.

Con: The questions.

First of all, the question you should never get is "are you pregnant," because by the time this book comes out, I assume some form of civil rights legislation will have passed making asking a woman that question a hate crime. But you might still get other absolutely ridiculous questions and comments that you will have to be prepared to answer while pregnant, so I've decided to help.

Q. You are so big, are you having twins?"

A. *"No, it's just one boy, but his penis is huge."*

Q. "Are you going to breastfeed?"

A. *"You know, I've tried it, and I'm just not that into it, but my mom has huge areoles, so it may just be a texture thing. I won't rule it out if I'm drunk, though."*

Q. "Wow, you're really eating for two."

A. *"Actually, I'm eating for ten. I have a tapeworm and I'm infested with botflies."*

Q. "If it makes you feel better, you don't look pregnant at all from behind."

A. *"That actually doesn't make me feel better, because babies don't come out of your anus, and it's unsettling to me that you think they do."*

Q. "You're still pregnant? It seems like it's been forever!"

A. *"I've decided not to have this baby until gay people can get married in every state."*

Con: The labor.

Prior to giving birth, especially in the final few weeks, you experience a desperate need to eject the baby from your body. You are swollen, your back hurts, your labia lips ache, and every time you take ten steps, you put your hands between your legs fully expecting to find a leg dangling there. You yearn for labor as a means of relief, and in your head and those marathon episodes of *A Baby Story* on TLC, labor is going to be a magical event where your cervix becomes the embodiment of the soul of Mother Nature, your insides twisting and turning to release this new force of life into the world.

The reality is that labor is pretty fucking terrible for about 90 percent of the population; the other 10 percent are either high or lying to themselves. In the old days, men used to drop the women off at the door, and then go chill in a cocktail lounge somewhere while their wives were put under using ether and then woken up after the baby was all cleaned up and their hair was freshly curled. What happened to that brand of medical chivalry? Now, due to advanced science and iPhone cameras, we're awake and present enough to experience everything. There are a few ways you can make the experience more bearable, like breathing exercises and epidurals, but I didn't go to any childbirth classes and it turns out, after my throat closed up and I began projectile vomiting, I'm allergic to epidurals.

Natural childbirth is a little bit like going down in an airplane: you have absolutely no choice, there is nothing you can do, your course has been set. Unless you are a pilot or a magician, the plane will crash and the baby will come out of you, one way or another. All you can do is lie there on your double-sided puppy pad and pray you are able to come out of it alive. You might scream at your husband, shit on the table, and hear your vagina skin tear in the process, but with God, your OB, the hospital maintenance guy in there fixing the television static, and the gaggle of interns as my witness, you will.

Pro: The baby(s).

At the end of everything, they give you a baby. It doesn't make you forget all the crappy stuff, that is just bullshit other parents feed you because they are desperate for company, but it's a fair enough prize. I liken it to getting a tattoo. It's scary and it hurts really bad, but when it's over, you are high on euphoria and desperate for another.

AFTER BIRTH

Andy and I went on to live through childbirth three times, and by the time we'd brought our third baby home, we pretty much had the whole newborn life down. On a physical level, nothing is the same after you give birth. I walked around like a slowly deflating balloon wearing mesh panties stuffed with adult incontinence pads in an effort to contain the endless blood that was gushing out of me. Everything was sore. My vagina looked as if I'd given birth to an adult bald eagle, feetfirst. I couldn't even wipe myself, but rather squirted my gentiles with warm water from a squeeze bottle after peeing.

In fact, you aren't even supposed to have sex until you are six weeks postpartum, but we ignored that the first time around, and by *we* I mean *Andy,* who took advantage of my weakened post-pregnancy alcohol tolerance and assured me he'd googled that if you were breastfeeding, getting pregnant was impossible. Long story short, I went to my six-week postpartum doctor's appointment two weeks pregnant. I had Wyatt almost eleven months to the day after I had Jude. Lesson learned: respect the six weeks. Gigi came two years later.

On a mental level, life begins to resemble a minimum security prison once kids come along. There are curfews, the food is questionable, and there are strict rules in place to prevent relations as well as emotional outbursts, both between and Andy and me, and the three screamy, full-diapered midgets we now cohabitated with. We've gone on to witness many of our friends' marriages break down over the stress and emotional turmoil of new parenthood, and we'd successfully avoided that by spending the six weeks post-baby living like a couple of dudes. I just pushed a baby out of my vagina. A whole baby. Followed by an entourage of umbilical cord, cottage cheese stuff, blood, and a placenta the size of a roast. I was unable to sit without crying, pee without screaming, or poop without biting down on a leather strap. And I don't want to discount the post-traumatic issues Andy dealt with having witnessed a baby climb out of me a few times. He once asked me to sit with him while he threw up rum in a hotel in Can-cún. I told him I couldn't because if I saw him puke, I wouldn't be able to kiss him on the mouth the rest of the trip. He's clearly a better person than I.

The six weeks of doctor-ordered celibacy was a time to focus on keeping the children alive, fed, and clean. After the first time around, we learned the last thing we needed was another baby in the mix, so we kept our pants zipped and didn't worry about squeezing in sex to meet a quota or even looking attractive for each other. In fact, aside from the occasional fist bump or bro-hug, we barely touched. This meant I never felt bad about dressing like an asexual high school softball coach, and Andy was kept at enough of a distance that he never rubbed up against the embarrassingly high elastic waistband of my granny panties.

You don't need frivolous things like sex or romance clouding up your already frayed judgment during the newborn phase. I have very vivid memories, or as veterans call them, flashbacks, about sticking a pillow over my face and screaming into it as I lay in bed, awoken again by the cries of the baby in the bassinet beside me. And if you thought having friends before kids was hard, once the baby arrives, your ratio of friends is directly proportionate to the number of unstained nursing shirts in your drawer. None. I had none friends. At least none that weren't reliant on me for survival. It's actually hard to be best friends with an infant; aside from them looking kind of like you and being able to put your nipple in their mouths, you have nothing in common. And it's mostly a one-sided relationship. You give them everything, they give you, occasion-ally, a smile that was probably just a prelude to shooting shit out of the back of their diaper. Yes, yes, there is the sense of completion and wholeness, but they don't get your jokes, they don't want to watch *America's Next Top Model* with you, and they don't care about the fight you just had with your husband.

At the end of six weeks I made my way back to the doctor for a full check, some oohing and aahing over baby photos, and a formal declaration that I was once again open for shop. News I cautiously brought home to my awaiting husband who sat desperately on my bed and watched as I packed up my maternity underwear, perineum bottle, and witch hazel pads one final time.

RHYMES WITH BAHSECTOMY

"I love having children with you. It's just that I'd like to not do that anymore," I explained to him in the booth of an Outback Steakhouse at the halfway point of our eighteen-hour road trip to visit his parents in Florida.

It's a tricky thing, you see. Telling the person you love that you'd no longer want to clone them in any fashion, ever again, because you've simply reached your limit of versions of their existence.

"I love you," I assured him, "but I'm finished."

Relief spread across his face, and we smiled together in the warm and affordable knowledge that never again would we be making another baby. Shortly after that, an infant cried from across the restaurant and my breasts started to leak. Yes. We were finished.

What followed was an aggressive game of "not it." Due to my fear of hormone medication and his distaste for latex and jerking off into socks, we decided to take a surgical approach to birth control. I was initially confused about his fear and the stereotypes surrounding vasectomies. I get that any instance in which his balls are handled in a nonsexual context is unpleasant, but *I* get my junk handled all the time, sometimes by doctors, sometimes by clumsy medical students, and sometimes by nosy dogs on the street. Getting my tubes tied is invasive and would leave Andy as the sole caregiver to three very small and demanding children if something happened to me. I'd like to think he thought about the consequences of each option thoughtfully, but honestly, I think he was just afraid to be alone with our children. Andy was getting a vasectomy.

Love had brought us to the outpatient surgical center at 7 A.M. on a Tuesday. It was love that helped me check him in with a three-month-old baby on my hip, and sit in the pre-op room with Andy as his eyes grew heavy and the small old nurse sat between his bare legs in stirrups, gently shaving his testicles. It was love, and probably the general anesthesia, that made Andy not run screaming half naked and bare-balled out of that building that day.

It was also love that I felt as I sat teary-eyed in the waiting room, surrounded by an odd influx of Mennonite people there, for what I assume was a very different reason. In a few short moments, having babies would be done for me. No more peeing on sticks, or baby kicks, or picking out names. I felt old and menopausal at twenty-eight, an age by which many women aren't even married or procreating by.

"Mrs. Gibbons?" the woman in scrubs called from the far hallway.

I looked up, briefly fearful that my mother-in-law had shown at to his vasectomy. No, wait, she meant me. Andy was out of surgery, and they had wiped away our fertility faster than it took me to peel the sticky glue from the back of a gift card. As I walked down the hallway to the recovery room, my ovaries played taps.

We had made this decision together, but I hadn't expected the sense of finality to it all. Being a mom was going to be my greatest accomplishment and my definition of success in this world. I had found someone to love me despite my garish physical flaws and I had gotten married and I had produced three children better than myself. That alone could be my livelihood. While I may never go on to do anything greater than Jude, Wyatt, and Gigi, I would still go on to do great things because of them.

11

THE FOURTH TRIMESTER (THE WORST TRIMESTER)

"I'M SORRY, I just can't do this right now."

"We've done it while you cried before; remember on the couch after *War Horse?*" he asked.

"No, it's not *War Horse* tears. I'm crying because I feel gross."

"I think you look hot," Andy assured me as he ran his hand down my back. I quickly pulled away, afraid he'd feel the line where the shapewear dug into my back fat. I'd been spending entire days in spandex tubes engineered to suck things in and push things down. I hadn't felt the natural skin of my stomach since having Gigi, not to mention that I was probably poisoning myself internally with carbon monoxide because I hadn't fully exhaled in months.

"I don't, I just feel disgusting right now, like my whole body," I sobbed.

"Well, don't I get a say in this?" he pleaded.

Gosh, I don't know. My initial reaction was to scream, *You sure don't, asshole!* But he wasn't trying to be a selfish jerk; he just didn't understand. Sure, I could just suck it up and have sex, but I'd be checked out and too consumed with worrying about what was jiggling, slapping, and drooping. My husband could tell me I'm beautiful until he was blue in the face, and it wouldn't make a difference because I didn't believe it myself. Hell, I barely believed it before kids, and I especially didn't believe it after.

Many women don't like pregnancy, but I enjoyed it all three times. I am curvy by nature, so the curves and swells exaggerated by pregnancy felt authentic and earned. Instead of walking around in public feeling unwelcome and judged, there was relaxed ease in my step. I could stand in the book aisle and place a hand on my stomach and instantly assure everyone I wasn't just big, I was pregnant. Someone thought I was wonderful enough to procreate with; how amazing is that, everyone?

Unfortunately, my postpregnancy body was like making a chubby woman out of silly putty, sticking your finger into the bottom of her throat, and pulling straight down. My body hung on me like and oversize padded jacket. Everything drooped and pooled into my dimpled thighs; I wore my stomach around my hips like a skirt, and my boobs pointed south. I had somewhat gotten used to the large body I had been carrying the first two decades of my life. I didn't like it, but I understood it. Postpregnancy, everything had moved around and redistributed to new fat areas, and I struggled dressing and accepting a new body. On top of the exterior issues, there were some added interior flaws as well.

My vagina was like an empty grocery bag.

I peed all the time: when I laughed, when I sneezed, when I ran. I once threw up so violently during a bout of food poisoning that my tampon shot out of me like a Nerf bullet. My vagina had the muscular makeup of those two hand-puppet Martians from *Sesame Street*. Out of necessity and lack of unlimited access to dry underwear, I began wearing panty liners full-time. Kegel exercises felt weird and unnatural to me, and every time I tried to do them, my right eye reflexively closed, my lips went numb, and I got a headache. My gynecologist insisted that I must be doing them wrong, and mentioned surgery to tighten my vaginal wall. Needle-shy, I opted to give the third option she mentioned, Ben Wa balls, a try.

Ben Wa balls are small metal balls you insert into your vagina in the hopes that the mere act of keeping them up there will tighten the muscles, making you better able to control your bladder and feel tighter during sex.

"Just put them in and go about your normal day," my doctor said with a smile after repeatedly assuring me that they wouldn't get lost inside my body and float up to my brain. She was looking at me like I was crazy, but she apparently has never had to fish out a lost tampon string while squatting over her grandfather's toilet.

I ordered a set online from a sex toy website and when they arrived I followed the instructions to coat them with lube, slip then in, and then proceed with life as they effortlessly strengthened my pelvic floor. I folded laundry as Andy napped on the bed, and I was careful to not move too quickly or cough them out. As I stepped to the side to grab more hangers from the closet, the balls slipped right out of me onto the floor. Thinking that perhaps I hadn't had them in far enough, I picked them back up, picked off the cat hair, pushed them back in as far as they could go, and penguin-walked back to the basket of clothes on the bed. See, they worked perfectly fine as long as I didn't move my legs apart.

"What are you doing, why are you walking like that?" Andy sat up from the bed as I was wobbling my way back from the closet.

"Nothing, go back to sleep."

"Seriously, what are you doing, you look ridiculous?"

"Nothing. Jesus, stop stalking me," I snapped.

"Just move your legs apart," he insisted.

I stood glaring at him from the entrance to our walk-in closet and slowly moved my thighs apart. There was a series of weird puckering sounds, and with a light thud, the balls once again dropped to the floor.

"Did you just shit on the carpet?" he screamed.

"No, God! They are exercise balls for my vagina; do we have no boundaries anymore?" I cried.

These things are either total vagina snake oil, or I've given my pelvic floor way too much credit. For now, I'll stick to Always with wings.

I can't feel my nipples.

I don't know if it's because I let three babies gnaw on them for a few years, or what, but I could get a nipple piercing right now and not bat an eye. Which is unfortunate because Andy rather likes to play with my nipples, and letting him do so often requires an Oscar-level performance on my part to keep his ego in check.

"Oh yes, baby, my nipples are getting so hard," I moan, with no actual knowledge of what is happening below my second chin.

My breasts sit lower, in general. Going braless is no longer an enjoyable act. Gone are the days of getting in my car after work and taking my bra off through my shirt sleeves to drive home braless with the windows down. Now when I stand in my closet and release the hooks of my bra, my boobs fall like gym socks full of quarters in a piñata. Leaving them loose is hot and hurts my back, so I look for support not only around the house, but even when I sleep.

I can't remember anything.

There is a kitschy term for this on parenting websites: it's called Momnesia. In short, I forget all the shit: appointments, meetings, that I'm walking around in public with depilatory cream on my upper lip, everything. And it doesn't go away as your kids age; the things you forget just get more important. Like what time school ends, where I parked my car at the airport, my wedding anniversary, or how the self-checkout line at the grocery store works.

Weight gain.

Well if this isn't the ultimate fuck-you. First I gain weight while growing the actual baby, and now that it's over, I keep putting it on. You know those women who brag they lose weight during breastfeeding?

"I didn't do a single thing. The more I nursed the weight just fell right off, and now I'm smaller than I was pre-pregnancy!"

I wish they'd die. I was only able to nurse my first two, Jude and Wyatt, for a short period of time, on account of getting pregnant again and having low milk supply. Therefore, I took full advantage of nursing my third child, Gigi, for eleven months, and I put on thirty pounds doing it. I attribute this to the fact that breastfeeding made me ravenously hungry and all my waking hours were spent sitting on my ass nursing my baby. I don't recall even standing upright until she had her first sippy cup of whole milk.

Hemorrhoids.

Go big or go home! That was my mental response to childbirth. You want me to push? Okay, awesome. I'm going to push so hard that I not only eject this baby from me, but I'm also going to turn my butthole inside out. When

I explained the issue to my OB, she insisted hemorrhoids were totally normal, and if they didn't go away, I could get a quick surgery to correct them, a suggestion that I met with a resounding "Nope!" I had already spent a month in elementary school sitting on a blowup pillow, and I'm not pulling my pants down as an adult to have surgery in my butt. So, here I am, five years out from my last birth and sitting in my chair a quarter of an inch taller.

IS MOTHERHOOD SEXY?

I was not in a good place physically, with my body, and mentally things were just as bad. I was having trouble rectifying my mom self with my woman self, which is insane because what's not womanly about walking around carrying a baby while you pee yourself and bleed from the ass?

My woman self spent a lot of time telling me that I should get dressed; put on a bra with underwire and jeans without an elastic maternity panel. My mom self reminded me that none of those things were practical, and that it was self-indulgent of me to worry about them when I had kids to raise. Beauty, sex, my marriage, myself . . . I pushed it all down hoping it would still be there by the time my kids moved out and I could afford liposuction and vaginal rejuvenation. I thought ignoring those things would make me a better mom. But the truth was, I was a mediocre mom at best. Obviously, my kids would disagree and tell you I'm fucking brilliant, but from where I stood, I was miserable and insecure with myself, and that was projecting onto everything I did.

I stopped being in pictures with my kids. If you were to flip through our family albums, you'd assume Andy was a single father. I hid behind the lens, pretending it was a fascination with my new camera, but really, it was fear of being photographed. The fastest you will ever see me run is after getting a notification I've been tagged in a photo on Facebook.

I stopped spending money on myself. As a mom, that is something we can all relate to. I'd do without and show up at a school event looking like a hobo if it meant my child looked stylish and adorable. I sidelined my own self-care to focus on my kids because I didn't look good in anything anyway. A low point for me was when I opened my underwear drawer to realize I didn't own any underwear that wasn't maternity underwear, and my youngest was three.

And I stopped having sex with my husband. Not only because I felt unattractive, but because sexiness was a womanly characteristic and I was too busy being a mom to be a woman. I wasn't able to balance the two, and I wasn't sure I was supposed to.

Then, the other day I received an email asking me if I thought motherhood was sexy. I laughed wondering if my kids would describe me as sexy to their friends.

"Hey, Wyatt, which mom is your mom?"

"Oh the tall drink of water over there with the messy red bedroom hair and giant tits."

The email ended up being an ad for a local pole dancing class, which I deleted because it combined two things that I hated: taking my clothes off in front of others and lifting my own body weight. But it did make me think. Of all the instances in life I was supposed to be sexy, I had assumed this whole time that motherhood would be one of the times I could tap out. To me, motherhood felt practical, like I was built for efficiency and snuggles and that's it.

They don't teach you in parenting books how to sensually fish a booger out of your daughter's nose with your pinkie. It wasn't erotic when the giant vein bulged out of my forehead as I whispered death threats to my tantruming children in the checkout line at Target. I don't even think the alluring scent of my pheromones made a dent in the thick layer of sticky foreign body fluid that coated my skin each day. I felt like the people who find motherhood sexy shouldn't be near children, or within one hundred feet of schools.

Looking back, I never thought of my mom as sexy. I thought of her as soft and familiar and low maintenance. I never looked at the other moms at my kids' school in their matching cardigans and thought, *Yeah, I'd fuck them.* When I did see a stereotypical "sexy mom" it was in movies like *American Pie* or on episodes of *Cops* wearing tank tops that said "MILF." Good moms weren't sexy moms. Good moms had snacks in their car and carried Vera Bradley bags covered in buttons with their kids' sport photos on them.

This is a burden of responsibility and martyrdom that is placed solely on the shoulders of mothers. Pardon my feminism, but was Andy getting emails with tips for how to make fatherhood look sexier? Probably not. Romantic comedies and yogurt ads dictate that we swoon over men who are good with children and pets. Even if they are just doing the exact shit we women do every single day, but for some reason, when we do it, it's invisible, and when they do it, it's a Hallmark commercial.

"Did you see how excited your husband was to watch Gigi dance in her tap recital? It was so cute!"

"I did, actually, and it was way sexier than the way I sat in the waiting room of the un-air-conditioned dance studio twice a week with thirty other moms shimmying four-year-olds in and out of full-body leotards to go to the bathroom."

As moms, the odds are not in our favor. Just look at all the lame stigmas attached to things with the word *mom* in it.

1 **MOM HAIRCUT.** After my second son, Wyatt, was born, I cut off my hair. It had hung down below my shoulders, and as

an act of motherhood compliance, I cut it off in the name of ease and convenience.

"You'll be so glad you did it," my mom assured me. "You'll wish you'd done it sooner."

Short hair and the removal of my dangling boho earrings and favorite perfumes and body sprays were just some in a long list of body modifications I made in an effort to be a more efficient model. I was subtracting things that made me feel beautiful and feminine in order to be a mother. Andy gave up dairy once, but that was because it was making him feel gassy, and it only lasted about a month. I cried every day until my hair grew out, and I haven't cut it since.

2   **MOM JEANS.** When President Obama threw out the first pitch at the Major League All-Star Game wearing smart light washed jeans that sat comfortable above the hips, he was endlessly mocked for leading the free world in a dowdy pair of mom jeans. Because for some reason, jeans with a rise that hit above your belly button are considered matronly and mom-ish. I say, bring it. The higher I can yank the waist, the more the jeans act as a second pair of Spanx. You're probably thinking, *Whoa, Brittany, what about camel toe?* Relax, guys, the maxi-pad I wear every day to catch the pee that shoots out when I laugh or sneeze eliminates that problem altogether.

3   **MOM JEANS.** The drop off and pickup line at my kids' elementary school reads like an anthropological study on motherhood. There are the twelve-passenger vans, you know, typical Catholics. There are the SUVs driven by moms who insist they are still trendy and pretend that it's totally not hard to cram three car seats onto a single bench, or, you know,

what I drive. And then there are the mom vans. Mom vans are minivans often as identical as the homes on a cul-de-sac, distinguishable only by the variations of stick-figure families on the back window and the blinking of lights from the keyless entry. These vans are loaded with DVD players and amazing features like sliding doors that open automatically and a tailgate that lifts when you wink at it; everything you need to make your life as a mom effortless and enjoyable. Except that driving one comes with the stereotype that you're old and enjoy missionary sex through the open zipper of your Ann Taylor LOFT capris.

4   **SOCCER MOM.** If you were to pop my trunk right now, you would find, admittedly, fast-food wrappers, half-empty bottles of water, and lots of clothes. But intermixed with all of that, you'd also find two soccer balls, a bag of football cleats, a couple of packages of emergency juice boxes, and two collapsible lawn chairs. If we were driving in a remote area, and our car broke down leaving us stranded, we could survive for days on the sustenance contained in the back of my SUV. We once drove Andy's car to a soccer game, and I watched him put two left shoes on our kid and deliver an after-game snack of unfinished Mentos. Soccer moms are the pack mules of parenthood. It's why they keep trying to make us drive vans.

Maybe finding the balance between sexiness and motherhood was hard for me because I wasn't confident with the sexy part to begin with, and the line between the two was often blurred between the screaming children and endless homework.

"Do you think I'm sexy?" I asked Andy as we sat in a booth during a rare date night at our favorite sushi restaurant, Kyoto Ka.

"Of course," he answered, not taking his eyes from the giant hockey game happening behind my head.

"Do you think I'm sexy when I'm being a mom?" I pushed again.

"Well, when *aren't* you being a mom?"

And that, friends, is a bit of truth right there. I was always being a mom. Andy had defined roles in his life. He was an engineer when he left the house each morning to go to work. He was a partner every Tuesday evening at his golf league. Andy was a dad when he came home from work and a husband when I needed him to kill a spider, and I mean that all in the best of terms. Andy was really good at compartmentalizing his life. I was not. I work from home, so the separation between writer and mother is blurred by the open door of my office, which ensures motherhood is a hat I can never take off. Even as I sat there on a date, I was gathering the stray straw wrappers into a pile and pouring soy sauce into our dishes. I was momming Andy out of familiarity and exhaustion, and as a result, I didn't feel like Andy's sexy wife or a strong, empowered woman. I felt like Nana from *Peter Pan*.

"I need to feel sexy in a nonparent capacity," I admitted, lowering the zipper of my hoodie and exposing more of my cleavage.

"I agree," Andy said, suddenly interested in the conversation. "It's a little emasculating when you cut my meat for me."

"Well, I like when you call me mama, but only when you make it sound telenovela exotic and not *Dora* exotic." I laughed.

"I don't like when you spell out sex words," he countered. "Or when you finish first and you cheer me on in the same voice we use to get Gigi to go in the big potty."

"Yeah, that's messed up." I exhaled into my beer. "Also, I know the wet spot in our bed is probably just apple juice, but for a second, I'd like to pretend it's not."

Can motherhood be sexy? Yes. Did I feel sexy? Not yet. But my lack of sexiness was not mutually exclusive to motherhood. I had forgotten how to be an actual woman who puts on makeup, cleans her vibrators, and deserves to like herself separately from the success and failures of those she cares for each day.

12

DAUGHTERS: THE ULTIMATE MIND FUCK

I THINK MOTHERS have an innate response to protect their daughters from low self-esteem. The problem is that they don't always have the tools or wherewithal to do it. Sometime after my father's accident, my mother went through this thing where she cut off all her hair, bought lots of knee-length cargo shorts from the men's department, and started breeding cocker spaniels. Or as it's called today, going butch. It was like she knew her life had changed and she was going to be suddenly carrying the roles of both father and mother. She took an equally masculine approach to my body image and tackled most of my concerns with an "eh, fuck 'em" attitude. Today at thirty, I can nod my head in agreement and put my fist in the air and yell, *Yes, fuck them all!* But as a teenager, reading *YM* magazine, watching MTV, and putting up with kids making farm animal sounds at me in the hallway, that fuck-'em attitude was a little harder to come by.

Realizing she was ill-equipped to handle the task, my mother decided to outsource my self-esteem issues by enrolling me in the prestigious Margaret O'Brien's International Modeling Agency. I would also like to add that Katie Holmes attended this exact same elite school before becoming famous for making Tom Cruise look creepier.

Margaret O'Brien's International Modeling Agency was in a run-down business park in South Toledo between a Kinko's and an office rented out for AA meetings. The only thing international about the place was the Hyundai parked out front and the fact that the lobby smelled like body odor.

Margaret O'Brien was an old woman with short dyed auburn hair, fake eyelashes, and long earlobes that drooped under the weight of her giant gold costume earrings. For more than forty years, Mrs. O'Brien had been running what was originally billed as "An Etiquette and Manners School for Fine Young Women," but now focused on launching the careers of future catalog models and wannabe Disney stars. She welcomed my mother and me into her office, and clicked her tongue as she went over my admission forms.

"It doesn't have your weight on here?" She looked up from the stacks of paperwork now spread across her desk.

"Oh, I haven't been to the doctor in a while, so I wasn't sure what it was," I lied.

"No matter." She stood up from her desk and walked around to my seat, reaching her hand out to me. "Give me your wrist. I can tell you everything you need to know about your body from your wrist."

I hesitantly put my wrist into her open palm.

"Do you see this?" she asked, showing me the tips of her cold, bony fingers wrapped around my wrist like a bracelet. "My fingers can't touch each other, that is how big your bones are, you will always be this big; nothing will change that, so you might as well get used to it," she said dismissively. This should have been a reassuring concept. I wasn't fat because I ate too much and wasn't active enough; I was big because my bones were big, and that is something you just can't control. But, because I was a teenager lacking the logic to understand that not every use of the word *big* in relation to my body was a bad thing, I took my large bones to be yet another personal failure.

Mrs. O'Brien was not in the business of turning people away, no matter how unsellable they were, so despite my giant bones, I was placed into the beginner's course for Confident Modeling, an exclusive course open only to people willing to pay the fee to attend. It was a rigorous six week program that culminated in a "professional" modeling photo shoot and fashion show in front of family and friends. Classes were focused on such topics as how to walk, how to behave in public, and basic hygiene. It was like going to school to learn how to be a well-mannered toddler, and many of the other girls in my class weren't far from that demographic. My classmates ranged in ages from seven to thirty-five; our only shared connections were excessive social awkwardness and ung-roomed eyebrows. None of us was what I would consider to be star material. We fumbled through posing lessons and overcom-pensated for our insecurities with loud, exaggerated horse clomps during runway practice. I wanted to tell my mom that I'd been shoved in the ugly class so that they could still take our money while pretending to make us feel pretty, but she'd spent so much, I felt horrible bringing it up at all.

Every Wednesday night I'd meet my mother in the parking lot after class, defeated and sore after the thirty-minute cheekbone-contouring marathon and having to squeeze my size 10 feet into size 8 heels.

"Do you feel prettier?" she'd ask, hopefully. As if that had been the point all along; if I felt pretty, I'd feel confident.

"I do," I lied, rubbing the balls of my feet and turning up the radio.

The night of the fashion show, I walked the runway in a purple beaded mother-of-the-bride dress with the matching ruched bolero jacket my mom bought for me on clearance at JCPenney. My parents clapped and when I got to the end of the runway, I silently mouthed the word *way*, just as my instructor encouraged us, so that our lips would be slightly parted and sexy in pictures. After the show, my mom and dad were waiting for me at the door with a bouquet of pink carnations and the envelope of "professional" head shots taken earlier that month.

"Now you can tell people at your school you're a real model!" my mom said excitedly from the front seat as we drove home.

"I'm not a real model, Mom. You paid an old lady money to take Polaroids of me in front of an oscillating fan."

I understand what my mom was trying to do. She didn't understand my confidence issues, because she didn't struggle with them herself. At least she didn't appear to. It wasn't that she walked around feeling gorgeous and untouchable, but rather, those weren't things that mattered to her, and she didn't understand why beauty and self-esteem had been things I was so hung up on. My mom had great intentions, but sending me to modeling class to feel good about myself was like enrolling someone who doesn't have any legs in figure-skating lessons; it just made me feel worse.

THE GIRL WHO SAVED MY LIFE

"She's a mini you!" they say, gushing over her big brown eyes and long thick hair as she spins in circles in the grass or sings complicated melodies of nonsense while dancing around the aisle in the supermarket.

And they are right. She has my eyes, and my wavy rebellious hair. She also has my thighs, feet, and lips. Gigi is witty and smart and curious and beautiful and I've spent five whole years nodding along with every relative, friend, and stranger on the street who told me she is exactly like me, even though I thought exactly none of those things about myself.

I woke up each morning and watched her dance in the sunlight coming through the curtains and thought, *Jesus, she is the most magnificent girl I have ever seen.* Sometimes my breath would even catch and my eyes tear up at her effortless joy and perfection.

And then I walked to my bathroom to get ready for the day and swore under my breath at the haggard and fat reflection staring back at me. Until one day it hit me. In a few years Gigi will stand in front of her own mirror, hating her own thick thighs and giant feet. She'll call herself fat and disgusting. She might even think, for a moment, that it would just be easier to not exist at all. I don't know what would destroy me more. The part that she could even for one moment think that she is anything other than beautiful, or the fact that she learned it *all from me*.

Of all the hobbies I have picked up and dropped over the years—the fiddle, magic, competitive eating—body hate has been my most dedicated and refined. And now with birth of just one tiny and beautiful girl, everything I knew about myself had changed.

Being a mother to boys has been completely different than being a mother to a girl. I love them all the same, that goes without saying. I would murder for them on a completely equal level, as well. There are just some things a little more terrifyingly relatable to raising a girl.

Some of them are obvious, like when Jude and Wyatt exclaimed during her first diaper change, "Why hasn't her pee-pee come in yet?" Or "Why does she have two butts?"

But the rest could only be picked up by a skilled eye. The way she'd linger in the bathroom to watch my nighttime routine, or stand in my closet as I picked out dresses for a night out. Unlike Andy, whose eyes glazed over when I would talk to him about clothes and makeup, Gigi would listen to me, wide-eyed, soaking it all in. It was momentarily lovely to have someone there to talk to. Until I realized that that someone was not my friend, but my very young daughter.

When they say you're not supposed to be friends with your kids, this is what they mean. All right, yeah, they also mean don't buy them beer and condoms and stuff, but more important, treating your little girl like a friend in place of actual friends is a terrible mistake.

One afternoon I watched her put on a fancy princess dress from her costume chest and walk to the mirror, frown, and touch her stomach in a way that brought me to my knees. She wasn't twirling or smiling or thinking about how sparkly and pretty she looked; she was mimicking the way I'd touch my stomach standing in front of the mirror, frustrated with my body and what it looked like in clothes, pressing my palm into my gut hoping to eventually just hit a reset button. I was not Gigi's friend at all. I was the woman ruining her life.

Looking my daughter in the face and telling her she was just like me, and in the next breath destroying my body in front of her, was a catastrophic mixed message. I was drowning in self-loathing, and the only way I could save her was to save myself. The problem was I had no idea how. I had been involved in a decades-long turf war with my weight, it's truly all I knew. I was able to completely ignore all the miraculous things I had done despite my size, and instead fixate on the scale. I had fallen in love, gotten married, had three healthy kids, and launched a booming career. I also never lost any friends due to my size, and to my knowledge, Andy has no plans to divorce me because I weigh over 200 pounds. The reality was that my life wasn't miserable because I was curvy; *I* was miserable because I thought I'd be happier if I were thinner, and when I sat down to think about it, it didn't really make sense. I was healthy and successful, all within the confines of this skin; so what if it made jeans shopping harder or airplane seats tighter? And even if for one second I was able to shut off the societal propaganda about how the better, thinner, half lives, how on earth could I ever convince myself that decades of beauty standards could legitimately be wrong?

Say it out loud.

Changing the narrative I supplied for my body was a very real fake-it-till-you-make-it scenario. I've never read *The Secret*. I am not a huge believer in hypnosis or positive thinking. My enthusiasm toward new-age hippiedom extends to almond milk and Nick Drake albums; that's it. Getting up each morning and saying three positive things about my body as I stood in front of a mirror felt silly and fake.

"My hair is pretty." (But I have two chins and my face is round.)
"My chest is sexy." (My stomach pooch hangs over my privates.)
"The area at the bottom of my ribs makes for a nice waist." (My legs are full of dimples and veins.)

My original goal here was to prove to a preschooler that I loved my body and that she should, too. But, as months passed and I stood grudgingly in front of the mirror, the positive affirmations were no longer followed by faults. In fact, I began to see less and less of them. I would catch my reflection in the car window or a security camera at the store, and instead of zeroing in on everything wrong with me, I began to only pay attention to the good. I did have great hair, my breasts were amazing and I had a really great waist and hourglass figure. I had talked myself into loving myself purely out of persistence and repetition. I still knew there were things about my body that I didn't love, but eventually, the good began to outnumber the bad.

Buy actual pants.

Listen, I love stretchy pants as much as the next person. And I make it a point to never judge other people based on what they are wearing, as long as it's not a Klan robe or a suit made of human skin. But for me, showing up at the store in leggings so thin you can see your cervix does not spell confidence, it spells resignation. I was in leggings because all my jeans were more comfortable in a ball on the floor than they were buttoned and on my body. I could buy bigger ones, sure, but if I did that, I'd be admitting to everyone that I'd gained even more weight, so instead I went through my late twenties riding a carousel of black stretchy pants; their level of formality determined by how faded they were.

"Does this look okay to wear to the funeral?" I asked Andy as he looked for a tie in the closet.

"Well, they're leggings, so . . ." He trailed off, unsure how seriously he wanted to debate the issue with me an hour before burying his grandmother.

"Right, but they are black," I said out loud, assuring both him and myself that it was a logical choice.

It wasn't a logical choice and I needed to go shopping, at the very least to get nonathletic wear to have on hand for funerals and church. What better way to show my daughter and myself that I was comfortable in my skin than to spend money dressing it in clothing that actually fit, just as I was, right in that very moment. Not after losing twenty pounds, not in the size I wished I was, but my actual real size. This was terrifying because I'd bought size 22 jeans once after having Wyatt, and I was so embarrassed by the size, I'd asked the girl at the register for a gift receipt so she wouldn't think they were mine.

I had to let go of the sizing issue, not only because there was no consistent standard, but because it wasn't an accurate representation of my body. I may have fooled myself into feeling proud I could button size 16 jeans, but I felt comfortable and beautiful in size 18, and I didn't have to unzip them once I got into my car.

Here is a secret: people can't tell what size you wear by looking at you, but they can tell what size you don't when your clothes are too tight. Let go of the number. In some stores I wear a size 14, in others a size 20. That insanity is on them, not my body; all I care about is having clothes that flatter me and don't leave indentations across my flesh. Once I learned that, for the first time in my life fashion became fun. I no longer left the dressing room defeated. I spent the time learning my proportions and shape, so that I was trying on clothing more likely to fit, as opposed to grabbing items based on what models who in no way shared my body type were wearing.

Fashion seems like a very superficial component of self-esteem, but for me it was the foundation. As a plus-size girl, trendy clothes and styles were often not on the table for me, so putting together pretty outfits was a whole new experience. Plus-size clothes were always less about style and more about comfort and utility. Stretchy jeans with elastic waists are really amazing, but just because we're chubby, it doesn't mean we don't have the hand-eye coordination to button pants. Making my way through the brands and racks, searching for pieces that fit well and were affordable, was tedious and laced with disappointment.

And that is where the confidence came in. I was taking the time to wear clothes I felt beautiful and empowered in, even though it was hard and time-consuming and I'm not the target demographic for many fashion designers. I was being fashionable and gorgeous in my body, not in spite of it.

Shut up.

A few months ago I was naked in the closet looking for clothes and Gigi came up to me, put her arms around my waist, and told me my stomach was big. Immediately I recoiled in horror and covered myself with the towel from my hair.

"Gigi, you can't tell people their stomach is big," I scolded her.

"Why not?" she asked, confused.

"Because it's mean."

"Why is that mean? I think being big is good."

And then it occurred to me that she had no idea that big meant fat, and that fat was a bad thing. As far as she is concerned, I'm just mom-shaped and perfect for hugs. I put a moratorium on the supply of negative body words I was thoughtlessly supplying. I banned the use of *fat* as a slur hurled toward myself and strangers. I'm not saying I don't see fat; saying that is akin to the people who make grand statements about "not seeing color." Seeing color doesn't mean you're a racist. It means your eyes work, but that you are hopefully able to see color not for a discrepancy in normal, but as a beautiful component of diversity. That's how I see bodies. They are diverse; some are skinny and some are fat. We can't all be Gisele Bundchen, but good heavens, can you imagine if more of you were? Think of all the XXLs that would be left behind for me at Target!

I stopped glorifying women as beautiful only if they were also thin. In fact, beautiful was the very last thing I decided I would tell Gigi she was each day, after brilliant, hilarious, curious, creative, and daring. There are so many important things to be in this world, it's unfair to devote so much of what describes us to our body size.

Get a sponsor.

My knowledge of sponsors and AA does not extend outside of *Nurse Jackie*, but I assume the basic premise is that when you think about drinking or you already have broken your sobriety, you call your sponsor for backup. I needed that exact scenario applied to my body image journey. Someone I could call when it was way easier to mentally beat the shit out of myself than to like what I was seeing in the mirror. I'm not talking about telling me I look pretty when I post a selfie on Instagram; I'm talking about the person I call at 3 A.M. when I've eaten everything there is to eat and everything inside me still feels empty and ugly, or when I don't feel like I'm even worth being seen with.

I'm here today because of my best friend, Shauna Glenn. I met Shauna while on a media tour in Boston and New York in 2009. Shauna was short and blond and looked like Britney Spears. I was tall, six months postpartum, and nursing a horrible bobbed haircut and an infant in a carrier across my chest. Our crude humor and sarcasm made us fast friends, and we stayed up late each night laughing as she bounced baby Gigi on her knee while I pumped cross-legged on the floor of her room. Later that trip she would also use a plastic knife to cut me out of a pair of Spanx in the hotel ballroom's bathroom after I couldn't get them off in time and peed my pants. Only real friends do that.

So, it was Shauna I called from my knees on the bathroom floor two years ago, the taste of blood still lining the inside of my mouth. She had always been the person I could text a fitting room photo to ask "Should I buy this?" or "Be honest, is this trashy sexy or trashy noooo?"

But she was also the person I called when throwing up every meal didn't take away all the horrible things people said about my looks and personality online or the way their words would seep from the screen into my head.

"Come to Texas," she insisted. "Let me take care of you."

She stood outside her white Jeep at the arrival gate of Dallas–Fort Worth airport with her arms open waiting to hug me. We spent the week under piles of duvets on her bed, watching funny movies and eating Mexican food. When we left the house it was to drive to Dallas to see indie films in empty theaters. There is heal-ing in feeling wanted and liked, and Shauna makes me feel both. She welcomes me into her home, lets me feel all my feelings, and then wakes me up the next morning with a tray of breakfast bur-ritos and Bloody Marys and tells me I look strong. I never fancied myself a Texas girl, what with my glaring liberalism and distaste for guns and secession, but Fort Worth has become my sanctuary, and Shauna my body sponsor.

> Take off your clothes.
> There are many things in life you cannot do naked. Like cook bacon or renew your driver's license. But when you are home, taking off your clothes and remembering what your skin looks like isn't an unreasonable request. I remem-ber getting out of the shower shortly after having our first son, catching my reflection in the mirror, and then scream-ing, convinced my mother was standing in the bathroom. It was me. I just had no idea what I looked like naked any-more.

I understand that if you have kids in the house, this can get creepy really quick, and it's hard to not want to cover your body around them before you're stuck answering questions about pubic hair and giant areolas. But if you can stand it, realize that it's important that your kids see your body the way it really is because it's helping build the normality of the way they see their own. Destroying the image that women are genetically born with well-groomed landing strips and airbrushed skin makes it that much easier for us all to stop seeing ourselves as failures. All of us shave our toes and that weird hair in our asses, and if you say you don't know what I'm talking about, you're lying.

Walking around after a shower naked is still not something I feel comfortable doing, but I do it to help put the standard bar for myself and my kids back at normal. You're welcome, future girl-friends of my sons with two different-sized boobs.

When I get on an airplane, I always listen to the safety instruc-tions the flight attendants recite before takeoff, mostly because I'm terrified to fly and I feel like if I listen carefully to the entire speech, whisper the Lord's Prayer, and stay awake the entire flight, I'll be able to keep the plane in the air. What I'm saying is, you are alive because of me, fellow passengers. My point is, once they point to all the exits and explain flotation devices, they get to this part about oxygen masks that drop from the ceiling should the cabin change pressure.

If you are traveling with children, or are seated next to someone who needs assistance, place the mask on yourself first, then offer assistance.

Even in a life-or-death situation, we are told to first secure our-selves in order to better help others. It makes sense. I mean, I can't put a mask on a baby if I'm passed out, and I certainly can't tell any-one to stop hating themselves while I binge and purge my feelings until my knuckles bled. Remind yourself of all the ways you are beautiful, stop the negative talk, get a body sponsor, and do what it takes to get comfortable in your skin. All of these were essential to help my daughter love the body I created for her. I just had to get my own oxygen mask on first.

13

LAST CAKE EVER

"NOTHING TASTES AS good as skinny feels."

Kate Moss has clearly never eaten at a Sonic.

I haven't talked a lot about dieting in this book, but I feel like maybe I should address it, because I'm sure you are wondering. A round girl like me . . . surely somewhere along the line it would have occurred to me that losing weight would be the sensible thing to do, so let's just deal with the literal elephant in the room so you can get back to the rest of the book without wondering why I didn't just strap on a lap band and get on with it.

FAT GIRL HERE FOREVERMORE

As my curvy sisters know, it's predictably easy for society to make assumptions about fat girls based on glossy magazines and romantic comedies. The poor Melissa McCarthys and Rebel Wilsons of the world are forced to forgo Oscar-inviting leads simply to dedicate a good portion of their screen time to laying the groundwork for the average life of a fat girl.

1. Spend one to two hours a day loathing yourself.
2. Explore binge eating.
3. Cut out pictures of thin models from couture ads and decoupage them onto your skinny-girl hope chest.
4. Fill hope chest with bikinis and midriffs.
5. Google fad diets.
6. Come up with zany plots to get a man to fall in love with you before actually seeing you in person, for example, online dating or the plot of a Dermot Mulroney movie.

The reality is that we're not all miserable unfulfilled losers, and we don't all have to be skinny. You can stay up until 3 A.M. to watch self-proclaimed doctors and experts preach to close-up camera shots of sad, impressionable fat people about the "metaphorical" sense of fullness eating your feelings provides, but those experts are liars. The fullness is not metaphorical, it's tangible. I can eat joy or sorrow until my belly button pops out like a turkey timer. I can stand naked in front of a mirror with my hands on my stomach and feel something where before there was nothing, and sometimes feeling full of something is exactly what you need, be it wisdom, shit, dicks, or eggrolls.

I hit the gym circuit pretty hard my freshman year of college. My roommate and I would set our alarms for 5 A.M. and pull ourselves out of bed to go to the fitness center across the street from our dorm. I'd wander unmotivated from machine to machine, completing the required actions and suggested repetitions. I'd look at myself in the wall mirrors spanning the length of the gym, dripping with sweat, and instead of feeling strong or accomplished, I felt exhausted and fake. I was just going through the motions of fitness alongside people who consumed it like communion at church. I feel more at peace eating a bag of licorice in my car in the parking lot of Target, which only goes to prove that you don't pick your moments of spiritual clarity and fortitude. You don't go looking for Jesus's face in a slice of toast, guys; it just happens to you.

Also, I'm choosing to save you my speech about how I think the government uses iPods to track fat people, and just say yes, I get it, we're all supposed to want to be thinner.

Being overweight isn't always a fun life choice. It's not enjoyable to go to the Gap with your friends and only be able to buy scarves. It wasn't delightful to spend summers at the quarry faking sickness or my period to get out of taking off my men's oversize crewneck to swim. It's not empowering to walk into a restaurant worried that you might not fit comfortably into the booth. Those aren't fun activities. I spent two decades wanting desperately to be skinny; the desire was always there. Telling a twenty-something girl she looks gaunt or like she might have cancer may just be the best compliment ever. Potato famine was the new black, and I would have traded my soul for a thigh gap, though if I had a thigh gap, I'd probably only use it to hold more snacks or not have to pay for a carry-on while flying Spirit Airlines.

Dieting was a trick I picked up from friends in college and it never went well for me. Wait, I take that back, I was an excellent dieter at 12 A.M. when I lay in bed upset at the marks my underwear was leaving on my skin. I fell asleep promising myself I would give up carbs for three months until I looked like Nicole Richie with giant boobs. But then I woke up, ate cold leftover pizza, and decided I would easily fix the whole problem by just not wearing underwear anymore.

BRITTANY'S CHRONICLE OF FAILED WEIGHT LOSS TACTICS

Last Cake Ever.

The day before I would begin a rigorous new diet regime, I would allow myself one final hurrah before hopping off the fatty train. I'd spend one last day devouring all the sweets and carbs in my house, for two very important reasons. First, they obviously wouldn't be around to tempt me anymore; second, it'd satisfy my cravings for all the food I shouldn't technically ever eat again. I'd take one final dance will all my unhealthy vices, gorging to the point where I'd collapse into bed sweaty and swollen, eyes dilated and mouth glistening, like I'd just returned from a heathen solstice celebration, and I'd never want to eat junk food ever again. I call this practice "Last Cake Ever," and I'd do it every time I woke up feeling fat in my pants. Sometimes I'd have three Last Cake Ever days in a row . . . I was way better at procrastinating than dieting.

Prescription diet pills.

This was one of my more death-defying stunts. My sophomore year of college I collapsed in the kitchen of my apartment, assuming I was having a stroke. I couldn't breathe or feel my lips or move my hands. I had trouble even remembering to swallow. My boyfriend rushed me to the ER, where it was determined that I was not having a stroke, but rather, a reaction to the Adipex and Diet Coke I'd been living on for over a month. I sat on the bed in a half-open hospital gown as a gentle nurse peeled the tape from the EKGs off my skin, and I swore I would never take diet pills

again. That promise lasted exactly three days, until I justified cutting them in half just to lose enough weight to fit
into a skimpy dress for my boyfriend's fraternity formal.
Predictably, I gained back all the weight after the prescription ran out, but not even a health scare or hospital copay
could deter me away from being skinny just long enough
to retake my Myspace profile picture.

Tapeworms.

I remember reading an article once about this Australian
cyclist who discovered he had a massive tapeworm when
he went to the bathroom and found a four-foot segment
of it hanging out of his anus. To the average person, this
is horrifying, but to a dieter, this sounds like a fun possibil-
ity. Is it gross to let a giant parasite hang out in your intes-
tines so you can drink and eat all you want with little to no
weight gain? I don't know, I lived with a girl half a semester
in college because her dad owned a Taco Bell franchise and
got us free burritos, so I wouldn't put it past me. Unfortunately, tapeworms have been surprisingly difficult for me to
get, no matter how much questionable sushi I eat.

Cleanse.

I am from the school of thought that you shouldn't drink
your food, unless you were just in some sort of horrific
accident that left you in a full-body cast with your mouth
wired shut—in that case then yes, blend up that meat loaf.
Otherwise, detoxing your body by living on juice and mon-
itoring your bowel movements is no kind of life; three days
in and I passed out in a Kroger next to where they make the
rotisserie chickens.

Weight Watchers.

The Weight Watchers program felt like the most youthful of the mom-diet trifecta, Jenny Craig and Nutrisystem being the equivalent of packaged MSG astronaut food. I don't want to say Weight Watchers is a cult, because that sounds like a bad thing and frankly, the members are so ride-or-die and they terrify me. It's more like a really dedicated sisterhood that likes to put food on scales and tricks you into feeling like a millennial with all their hip spokespeople and mobile apps. Whenever I talk to someone who's done Weight Watchers they always tell me about how it's not a diet, but a lifestyle change. Collecting points like mahjong was fun at first, but there's something unnatural about low-fat cheese product and skim milk. And they taste horrible.

No wheat/dairy/carbs/meat/gluten.

Giving up literally every food is the worst idea ever. My mind just can't forget that these things exist. As much as we may wish it to be true, "close enough" does not a potato or piece of bacon make. I've been loyally eating Special K for breakfast since Cher Horowitz in *Clueless,* and she was able to wear thigh-highs without having them roll down like exploded sausage casing. And now, all of a sudden, cereal and milk is bad? As if, America. As if.

The gym.

There is no greater motivation to join a gym than to see a photo of yourself taken from the back wearing an outfit you were sure you looked really good in. No matter how the commercials try to sell it, gyms have never felt like a comfortable and welcoming place for me. No one high-fived me or offered to spot me or explained the rules about what towels we can bring into the steam rooms. If I'm looking for a friendly place, I'll go to Chipotle. All of the workers smile when I walk in and say hi, and when I'm building my burrito, they treat me like an innovative genius, like the Steve Jobs of tortilla stuffing. Chipotle is like Cheers for chubby people; gyms are not. And I just want to add, you know, to put it out there, that people are allowed to not like the gym. It doesn't mean that I'm inactive or unhealthy; I just genuinely don't enjoy it. In the same way I prefer not to watch Tyler Perry movies.

Become an Asian competitive eater, motherfucker.
Aside from not being Asian, I really didn't see how this plan could fail. You just dip the hot dog in the water and put it in your mouth. I've watched many a thirteen-pound Asian girl out-eat ten men three times her size and still shop at Limited Too.

Just kidding; my hands would stink like hot dogs all day. That smell never washes off. Like gasoline, cat pee, or Shalimar in the rugs of the apartment you rented after that old lady died.

NOW WHAT?

My fitness and body aspirations at thirty are different from my aspirations at twenty. At twenty, I just assumed I'd work out until I was so tiny, people became concerned for my health and I'd roll my eyes at them from my Victoria's Secret bras and Abercrombie jeans. Now I just want to maintain my current weight so I don't need to buy new clothes. When you look at weight loss, it's often clothing driven. Weddings, vacations, and high school reunions, all things you are supposed to be thin for. But what if you have a gorgeous wedding dress in your current size, loads of flattering bathing suits, and a killer pair of jeans? Starving myself has suddenly become a moot point. I have options; I'm no longer a fashion pariah. So where does that leave my weight? Well, unless I'm sitting atop you, what I weigh is really none of your business.

I like to put good food in my mouth, and while I am aware of the calories I ingest, instead of cutting them I make them count. I have a full-on love affair with food, appreciating the different cultures and processes within it. In fact, I take entire vacations around eating. It's how I remember where I've been; I've either eaten, thrown up, or started my period without the proper supplies there.

Beignets with my best friend in New Orleans. Too much rum on the beaches of Playa del Carmen on our second honeymoon. Orlando, Florida, the city of emergency men's tube sock maxipads.

You see, these flabby parts aren't problem areas; they're parts of a scrapbook.

14

HOW TO BE PROFESSIONALLY FAT ON THE INTERNET

THERE IS NO greater motivation to be successful than being homeless. Okay not *homeless* homeless, but without home to the point you have no roof over your head and are forced to move your family of five back in with your parents and their nine pugs and get on public assistance.

You are probably thinking right now, this sounds weirdly like the life of J. K. Rowling, and I would agree. We live basically mirrored lives; she's a billionaire living in London writing about wizards, and I'm in Ohio famous for writing about my crotch and stretch marks.

I bounced a dark-eyed baby girl on my knee as we sat in the pale mustard-colored room of the downtown courthouse. The only window faced a brick wall, and I bit the inside of my cheek and focused on the rain running along the rusted metal pipes outside to keep from crying.

"I think we're the only ones who brought a baby to a bankruptcy hearing," I whispered to Andy.

"Well, we didn't have a sitter and I don't exactly know the rules," he snapped before softening and grabbing my hand in his.

Stuff like this wasn't in your vows. The officiant didn't ask me to say, *I Brittany, take you, Andy, to be my lawfully wedded husband, in happiness and in sorrow, in sickness and in health, in wealth and in the absolute humiliation that comes with bankruptcy, as long as we both shall live.* It's not that I wouldn't have committed to the vows, but a heads-up would have been nice.

We had been doing so well. Andy was working in IT for a large car manufacturer, and I was home with the kids, picking up part-time income from the advertising that ran on my blog on the Internet. We had bought our first home, a quaint yellow two-story farmhouse in the country that reminded me of the *Gilmore Girls,* and Andy traded in his sensible family sedan for a sports car that he leased on his twenty-eighth birthday. We hosted family Thanksgiving gatherings and Christmas morning brunches, took vacations, and sent our boys to private preschool. Andy and I were living the American dream I'd always wanted. No struggling, no stress, no empty stomachs.

Who could predict that an hour before I gave birth to our third child on April 30, 2009, breaking news would interrupt my labor and a TBS showing of *Clueless* to inform us that Chrysler had declared bankruptcy. And thirty minutes after that, Andy's phone would ring telling him that he, and thousands like him, no longer had a job. There was no work, no answers, no medical insurance, and no way my single income could support our new family of five.

"This baby cannot come out right now," I pleaded with the doctor whose hand was wrist-deep inside me.

She laughed uncomfortably, unsure if I was serious, and asked the nurses to ready the room for delivery.

"I'm serious. Andy, please," I begged Andy, clawing at his hand with every contraction, "Do something; we can't have this baby on the day you lost your job!"

I cried with every breath and every push, until finally our third child appeared, her cries in competition with my own guttural wailing. Just as we had built our lives on our own, accepting no help or handouts from Andy's wealthy family, we had lost it all on our own as well. It was a blow to our bank account, as well as our ego.

PUBLIC ASSISTANCE

I sat in the parking lot of the health department in my two-year-old navy Dodge Durango. I'd loved it because it was big and strong, and I felt safe and untouchable powering through the streets with babies in the backseat. It was my very first new car, and it held its own each day in the car line outside my kid's school, among the Escalades and the Hummers. Now it had taken me someplace very different: to the Fulton County Health Department to apply for public assistance.

You see, there is very little room for pride in parenthood. When you have three children and are living right at or slightly above your means, it takes almost no time at all to run out of money. Two months into Andy's layoff, bills began to fall behind and our meals became less frivolous and a bit more purposeful; meat for energy and carbs for fullness, the bulk of our money going toward diapers for the baby and whole milk for the boys, and even that grew tight. Eventually we had to ask for help.

WIC stands for Women, Infants, and Children, and it's an income-based nutritional supplement program for children and expecting or postpartum mothers. Upon acceptance, you receive a coupon book each month for milk, cheese, fruits, vegetables, and grains. I am not sure where conservative politicians get their information, but I can assure you there is no sense of ease or entitlement in government assistance. I wasn't a blip in the system or exception to the rule. I sat in the waiting room with three children at my legs, surrounded by parents who looked just like me: tired, down on their luck, and embarrassed. Once called back to the patient room, the children and I were questioned about our diets, had blood drawn to check our iron, and then weighed.

"Are you pregnant again?" the small blond nurse asked me as she adjusted the metal bar of the scale.

"No," I answered. "I always look this way."

There was no part of this process that wasn't humiliating, from having your life judged and documented by government workers to pushing your cart full of children and WIC coupons up and down the aisles of Walmart, looking for the kindest cashier with no line to check you out.

We were on WIC for eight weeks, and as the auto industry perked up, Andy eventually got his job back, but it was already too late. Four months was all it took to break us.

MR. AND MRS. CONNER

I'd spent the evening before our bankruptcy hearing packing up our belongings, nursing the baby, and watching marathons of *Roseanne* on Nick at Night. As a kid, *Roseanne* was a show I had trouble watching. It hit a little too close to home for me, and I swore I would never let my children grow up in a house where the lights were shut off or the refrigerator was empty. Andy joined me on the couch as I cried watching Dan and Roseanne Conner love each other fiercely, despite being down and out more often than not, with equal parts irony and inspiration. Bankruptcy was a moment. Walking into the health department for public assistance was a moment. Moving back in with my parents for a few months while we got back on our feet would be another, *oh my God long*, moment. These scary things we were going through were just moments in a life filled with millions of way more amazing moments, and we could either let them drag us down or we could stand up, use them, and keep on loving each other fiercely.

"Gibbons?" The clerk called from the doorway of the courtroom. "Mr. and Mrs. A. Gibbons?"

"After you, Mrs. Conner." Andy stood up and reached for my hand.

"No, after you, Mr. Conner." I smiled.

We sat across from a court trustee as he flipped through a binder of our creditors. Credit cards that we'd maxed out buying groceries and gasoline. Overdue water bills and disconnection warnings. The receipt of repossession for Andy's sports car, which had been picked up from our driveway only days before, me watching it being towed away from my front porch, my neighbors watching from their living rooms.

None of our creditors showed up to the court hearing, though they had every right to do so in an attempt to enforce payment of debts. Maybe in terms of the big picture, what we owed wasn't worth the trouble. Maybe they hated showing up to court to face poor people. Whatever the reason, I was thankful to look behind me and see only empty seats.

"Will you be keeping your home or surrendering it back to your mortgage holder?" the trustee asked softly. No matter how many times a day he was made to say this he was still careful to give it the pause and grief it deserved.

"We're giving it back," Andy responded quietly.

"Just sign here." He placed a paper on the table across from us and shoved two pens our way. Signing away our home was the last significant act of the day. I walked out of the courthouse broke and without a home.

If I learned anything from that experience, it was that I would never put myself or my kids in a situation where the loss of one job would destroy our lives. It was more than just making better choices or creating an emergency fund. I had become far too dependent on my husband, and for the first time in my life, I felt drive, ambition, and blind hunger for my own success and security.

I AM AN ADULT WHO WORKS ON THE INTERNET

I started a blog in 2007, after having watched a news story about a mommy blogger who quit her full-time job to write about diapers and cleaning products from home, for money. I had long since quit planning weddings at the country club, and was staying home with two toddlers at the time. The only opportunities I thought existed as a writer were working for magazines or publishing a novel, two things that felt very out of my reach without the degree or the time. But writing on my own terms online was an exciting notion. I'd always been tech-savvy, creating a GeoCities website in college and throwing myself in social networks and forums while the children slept.

I went to work building my site, never calling myself a "blogger," because that's a bizarre word (think: moist) and because in my opinion a blog is simply a medium. I'm a writer. I just happen to put my words on the Internet because it's the twentieth century and I've forgotten how to hold pencils. I've also forgotten how to properly fill out checks. Whenever I am forced to do it, I always end up having to google how to accurately spell out the numbers and I treat the "memo" section as a tiny to-do list that serves as a much-needed reminder by the time the bank mails the check back to me.

"Oh look, the electricity company cashed our check and I still haven't called about that blood in my stool, I'm on it!"

The very first blog I created was called Barefoot Foodie, reflecting my then status as a stay-at-home mom with grand visions of becoming a famous food critic or television chef. There were a few problems with this plan. The first as that the only restaurants close to my house were a McDonald's, a drive-through Subway' and a seafood restaurant, and it's really hard to critique shellfish in a landlocked state. Second, none of my recipes were healthy, and 2007 was the beginning of world domination for the vegan-gluten-paleo folk. And third, it was just a really sucky blog. I mean, there are only so many adjectives at my disposal to describe a bite of food, and eventually everything was just nutty and earthy and acidic.

"I can't put my finger on it, but this cut of steak almost has a nutty quality to it. Very earthy, and yet borderline acidic."

It was just gibberish. I didn't like to write about food, I liked to eat food, and that's not entertaining unless I'm doing it naked on a webcam and you're paying $9.99 a minute to view it. Which I would do, by the way, as long as it wasn't soup. I don't eat soup in front of other people, and I especially don't eat it naked.

After the demise of Barefoot Foodie, I began a two-year-long adventure of simply playing on the Internet. My sweet spot was always humor, so I would update the defunct food blog every few days with humorous anecdotes about marriage and babies, the two things I happened to be elbow-deep in at the time. And suddenly, people started reading it; real people, not just my mom and my therapist, Tom, who frequented my writing to look for cries for help. The posts were read and shared and shared again between women and work friends over coffee and in emails between sisters.

My readership grew larger and larger simply because other women were relating to what I was saying. It wasn't anything particularly poignant, but it was honest. Marriage was hard. Motherhood was hard. Remembering to be a woman through all of it was hard. There were so many examples of women online and on television flawlessly pulling off their lives—great clothes, clean living rooms, trendy children—that women began looking for someone to admit how messy and mistake-ridden it all really was.

I was crude and sloppy, entwining four-letter words with detailed exploits of my sex life and my periods. By the end of 2009 I had a monthly readership of over 100,000 as I wrote from the couch in the one-room garage apartment of my parents' home, and it kept climbing. I had outgrown the confines of the mom demographic and was being devoured by girls in college, empty-nesters, and husbands desperate to relate to their wives. Companies that had previously shunned me for my language and explicit content began buying ad space, attaching my name to campaigns and advertisements. I was making more money through my blog than I'd earned at any of my previous non-Internet jobs, and I didn't even have to put pants on to do it. I'd saved up enough for a substantial down payment on a house, and we moved out of my parents' garage into a large home in the country, and two years post-bankruptcy, I began to out-earn Andy, and it's been that way ever since.

For the very first time in my life, I had a career and I had a purpose and I was popular. I had built a huge community of readers, and they were emailing me, sharing their experiences and relating to my posts, even though in truth, I was functioning at a pretty anonymous level. Sure, they knew my first name, and saw me through carefully crafted and cropped photos on the Internet, but they were accepting my cockiness and confidence at face value. I wasn't either of those things in real life, and I couldn't talk about what was really happening, because it wasn't always hilarious and it wasn't always fun to read. I wanted to talk about the way my stomach made a slapping sound when I ran, the horrible things I said to myself when I put my jeans on, how disappointed I was in my size, and how some days I barely left the house because I hated what I looked like so much.

Just like high school, I lived in constant fear of outing myself as a fat girl, until one day, someone else did. It was a comment on a photo on Facebook from the baby shower of a fellow social media personality. I had carefully posed myself behind the mom-to-be and some of her friends, but despite the creative concealment of my body, someone left a comment declaring that I was too heavy for the outfit I'd worn. It was the first time I'd experienced shaming on the Internet because up until that point, I had controlled the discussion and characterization of my story. It was my safe place, and losing that terrified me. Side note: is anyone else grateful social media wasn't a thing when they were a teenager? It's like Draco Malfoy and all three Heathers smooshed into one invisible organism that thrives on Internet memes and passive aggression.

After some mean-spirited banter in the comments, the author must have had a run-in with her conscience and tried to remove her post, but it was too late. I'd read it and my heart dropped and my face burned and suddenly I was that girl in high school again trying to pretend I didn't hear it when someone called me a name in front of all my friends. The difference was that this time the feelings of shame and fear were overshadowed with absolute anger. I had already paid my dues as *that* girl. I was *done* being *that* girl.

I was tired of living in fear of someone telling the community I had worked so hard to build who I really was, and I was tired of hiding behind turtlenecks or conveniently blurry or cropped photos. That kind of fear is a full-time job, and I didn't have time for another one of those. I was going to own my body and the words about it from that point forward. I relaunched my website in my name as BrittanyHerself.com (all right not my actual name, but BrittanyGibbons.com was actually owned by a teenage country singer, and she refused to sell it to me, so I had to improvise) and used it as a platform to write not just about being married and raising kids, but about my struggles as a curvy woman, because after all, that is what every part of my life boiled down to. It affected the way I parented, the way I interacted with my spouse, the way people saw me, and the way I saw myself. I wasn't always a sarcastic and crude girl making dick jokes. I was 250 pounds and an insecure mess.

Through hiccups, tears, and one very large Frosty from Wendy's, I finally typed out the words I'd been too afraid to admit: that I was fat, and that I hated myself for it. Here is a glimpse at what I wrote:

> *I spend most of my day loathing my body, and sharing that with Andy is hard enough, let alone admitting to him that others see me the same way. Obese.*
> *I feel like I am just that much further from liking myself.*
> *I'll still look for excuses to change in my bathroom with the door locked, or hide my Spanx at the bottom of my underwear drawer, or act busy and hurry away when he tries to put his arms around my waist.*
>
> *I want to not spend so much time hating myself. But, it'd be a whole lot easier if people would stop reminding me about all the reasons why I should.*

YOU'RE NOT AS THIN AS YOU THINK YOU ARE

It turns out that once you admit to a community of readers that you are plus size and miserable they either say, "Ew, gross" or "Me too!" For every person who stopped reading my blog, I gained ten more. Plus the occasional chubby-chaser who inquired how happy and satisfied I was in my marriage and if I'd send them a picture of me slowly eating a box of doughnuts.

Job number one while being fat on the Internet is figuring out just how fat on the Internet you actually are. Yes, sure, I had a scale, I could read numbers, I knew how BMI charts worked, but I also had a mean case of body dysmorphia . . . in opposite-land. Meaning, I thought I was thinner and prettier in the mirror than I was in real life. It happens to us big girls at some point. You leave the house thinking you're having a good hair day and your jeans fit great, and then you catch your reflection walking past a store window and you decide none of those things is true and your brain is a liar. It's defeating and a million times worse when you have that realization in front of millions of readers on the Internet.

My very first press tour was a multicity campaign with Lands' End in 2010 for their swimsuit line. Lands' End was one of the first fashion companies interested in appealing to the "real woman" demographic, and they approached me about collaborating on their swimsuit confidence campaign. Without even considering the depth or ramifications of the project, I pitched a great idea that had me standing in my bathing suit in Times Square outside *Good Morning America;* they loved it, arraigned a bunch of interviews with various other media outlets, and flew me out that May. I was still very much a starry-eyed girl from Ohio at the time, so I showed up at my fancy hotel suite in New York City, with a king-size bed with clean sheets and freedom to crank the air conditioner as high as I liked, feeling very important and untouchable. Every day I crawled out of bed at 3 A.M. to dress myself decently enough to hail a cab and make it to a 4 A.M. call time for hair, makeup, and wardrobe at whatever morning show I was making my rounds to that day, and I never once worried about my stretch marks or back fat, because someone else was there buttoning my pants and shifting stuff around to make me look pretty. I smiled in the mirror and made my way onto the set confident and perky with blown-out hair and perfectly lined eyes.

Between satellite interviews about the confidence and empowerment that wearing a swimsuit evoked, I would waltz back to the greenroom to grab some food, and when one of the production assistants showed me a photo they had snapped of me on set, being all famous, I spit the bagel out of my mouth, locked myself in the bathroom, and commenced bawling my fake eyelashes off. That girl in the picture was not how I saw myself in the mirror. That girl in the picture looked like Shrek.

I pulled the poor confused production assistant into the bathroom and laid out the laundry list of flaws I'd seen in the grainy, poorly lit cell phone picture: the arm fat, the double chins, the hunchback. She swore that she saw none of those things, and promised me that the person I saw in the mirror was exactly the person everyone else saw, and even though she probably had way more important things to do, she spent the next ten minutes taking pictures of me so I could practice sitting until I found a position I felt I looked okay in. The irony is that prior to that moment, I had stood in my hotel room in my bathing suit in front of a full-length mirror and concluded that every step I'd taken to love my body after having my daughter was working. If I never lost another pound, I'd be totally okay because jeans looked cute, and shirts looked cute, and my hair was finally out of that super-awkward stage where it was annoyingly hovering around my shoulders to the point that I'd made all my friends promise not to let me cut it because doing so would only end in regret, much like when I get attached to shows that ABC eventually cancels without warning (I will avenge your death, *What About Brian*).

That media tour was a wake-up call to how I viewed myself. Naturally, I'm going to be harder on myself than others might be, but it was painful coming to terms with how I really looked on camera alongside the audiences of *Good Morning America, Connecticut Style,* and *The Daily Buzz.*

However, it inspired me to take the time to get to know my body. When I stood in front of the full-length mirror in my bedroom each morning, I was no longer just telling myself I was sexy and strong: I moving and posing my body, not out of narcissism, but in a quest to find poses that made me feel beautiful and confident. Hating yourself in pictures or in video is the worst. And may God smite anyone who posts a photo of you eating, because absolutely nobody looks attractive while eating. I practiced those poses every day so that the muscles in my body would remember them, and when a camera pointed was my way, my body naturally found those movements and I walked away from the experience confident that I knew how I looked. And with that confidence, the more I put myself out there, on television, on my blog, or Internet fetish sites, the more I could objectively handle the criticism and snark that were lobbed my way and be able to step back to say, "You know what, that's fair," or "No way, troll, you're full of shit, my body is made out of stardust."

TAKING CHARGE

The second rule of being fat on the Internet is taking charge of your fat on the Internet. There's a weird belief floating around that just because you are confident in your body, you don't care what it looks like in photographs or on-screen. And that by speaking up about how you want your body portrayed, you are somehow defeating the very platform you are promoting. That is bullshit, and I learned that the hard way.

In the early years of my blog, any media attention or promotion was a big deal; I took whatever I could get. So when I was contacted one week after giving birth to my daughter by a local paper that wanted to feature my site in a story about mommy bloggers, I naturally jumped at the chance. The male reporter asked me various eye-roll-inducing questions about how moms were turning to blogs for therapy, and why I thought the Internet was, you know, a cure for our lady hysteria. When he tried to arrange for a photo shoot in my home, I kindly offered to email him a head shot. Just like Jewish people sit shiva for seven days follow the burial of a loved one , there is an unspoken period of time after giving birth when women are allowed hide in their house in mesh hospital underwear, accepting casseroles at the door and not having to appear in photos. It is for this reason that the conversation with the reporter should have ended, but he pushed for the shoot and I was afraid saying no would cost me the story, so it was scheduled.

An old man with a camera came to my home eight days after I'd given birth to my third child and took a series of photos of me in my dark living room, as I tried to smile between corralling two small toddlers, quieting a newborn, and adjusting my breast-milk-soaked nursing bra. Frazzled, I had collapsed on the couch to adjust my maternity jeans when he snapped a picture.

"Just testing the light," he assured me.

That was the photo the reporter used for the story.

It's events like this that fuel me to put aside my fear and complicity, but as a woman, it's hard to be that vocal. It was hard to speak up and set the terms when I had absolutely no experience doing either of those things. I wasn't "leaning in" just yet.

A few years later, I would again find myself on the set of a daytime talk show, again in a bathing suit, and again talking about a piece I'd written about body confidence. The cameraman had positioned the camera at a very low angle, almost resulting in an upshot, which I think we can all agree should be illegal and punishable by nail gun to the throat.

"Excuse me," I said sweetly to the cameraman. "Is there any way you can aim the cameras down at me a bit more? This upward angle is really unflattering. It's a woman thing." I shrugged, trying to keep things friendly.

"Sorry, these cameras are set for the host, not you," he answered matter-of-factly.

And that's when I knew. I wasn't going to be the woman just lucky to be on the screen anymore. I was going to be the woman they set the cameras for.

CHANGE THE MOTHERFUCKING CONVERSATION

Body talk was becoming a huge topic across almost all forms of media, but unfortunately, the majority of it surrounded the effects of unrealistic beauty standards and bullying on teen girls. Having a daughter myself, I could see why these conversations were important, but what about the rest of us? What about the women who were being fat-shamed in the media, discriminated against in the workplace, mocked on television, and ignored by the fashion companies? Where was the guide on how to be thirty and plus size and love yourself? Where were all those conversations?

They weren't happening yet, leaving an entire population of women completely disenfranchised, and I saw this as a chance to become a point of reference and authority for plus-size women online. I was already speaking out about my weight and my struggles with body image, and was making huge strides not only in personally loving my size, but in helping others do the same, so that Band-Aid had already been ripped off. Now it was just a matter of turning the societal conversation from fat discrimination to body acceptance. Plus-size people were often portrayed in society as villains. We affected your health-care costs with our diabetes and our heart attacks. We all wanted gastric bypass and lap-band surgery as an easy way out. We were eating all the fast food from the dollar menu. We were lazy, lacked self-control, and were unpleasant to look at. We were an epidemic.

Plus-size people didn't want to hear that anymore, and more important, whatever anyone hoped to change with that kind of negative dialogue wasn't changing. Women especially wanted someone to stand up and say all the things they weren't brave enough to say yet. They wanted to talk about having sex and shopping and friendships and dating, not as a plus-size person, but as a *person*. We aren't fetishes or last resorts, but we were being treated that way in the media. Curvy women wanted to be reassured that they were allowed to both love and hate parts of their body and at the end of the day, still have worth.

So those are the conversations I started having. I denounced body shaming. I promoted loving your body, just as you were. I challenged fashion companies to step up to the plate and provide us with stylish options and realistic models. I grabbed my bathing suits and skinny jeans and talked about fashion that worked for my body. And I started taking my clothes off every chance I got; hell, I gave every sex worker in America a run for her money. The more people saw me, the more normal my body became to them. People see a naked thin woman and think, *Oh isn't she beautiful.* Then they see a naked plus-size woman and think, *Oh bless her heart, she feels good about herself, that's adorable.* I was going to keep showing the world my body until the reaction stopped being *how nice for her* and started being *look at that beautiful woman.*

This quest solidified me as the Internet's token fat girl, and I appeared on news shows and podcasts and was quoted in magazines, all because I was the authority on being fat. Something that years ago would have humiliated me, I now wore like a badge of honor. What's the worst that could happen? I'm called fat? My self-esteem was made bulletproof, and as a result, I'd become fearless.

SHE WORE A BIKINI ON THE INTERNET

Pushing the limits of the Internet is a necessary evil. In a space that welcomes robot porn and WikiLeaks, it's imperative to come off each accomplished project with a resounding "Now what?"

She talked about her sex life on the Internet, now what?
She revealed her weight on the Internet, now what?
She stood in her shapewear on the Internet, now what?
She wore a bathing suit on the Internet, now what?

In 2013, that *now what* became a bikini. It had been, easily, twenty-five years since I'd worn a bikini, but being caught up in the excitement of feeling sexy and strong and the Internet's siren calls of *now what*, it seemed like the next natural step.

This was no easy mountain to climb. It had cliffs and caverns and stretch marks and gallbladder surgery scars and love handles and saggy parts and a belly button that was so totally lower than I remember it being before. Oh, and a stupid amount of cellulite. But it turns out, putting on a bikini was so much harder than just, well, putting on a bikini. In fact, I had been so focused on the actual act, I never even considered the difficulty in finding one that fit. There is so much to consider, especially with a curvy body. I needed a bottom that came up high enough to hide my pouch, and a top big and supportive enough to handle my 38Hs. That made for slim pickings. Also, I'm not, like, sixteen years old, so there's that.

After taking to the Internet, because heaven forbid we plus-size gals try anything on in a store, I ordered an absolutely obscene amount of bikinis, took a few shots of tequila, lowered the air-conditioning in my bedroom to about 50 degrees (the temperature where my skin felt the firmest and I wasn't working up a sweat shimmying in and out of Lycra), and after forty-two or so emotional breakdowns on my bedroom floor and a case of alcohol poisoning, ended up with two that made me feel positively gorgeous.

Andy took the photos on a freezing February morning. Yes, Andy takes all of the fashion-related photographs on my website. If you would have witnessed this happening a few years ago, you would have seen me poring over his camera, explaining to him the importance of angles and downshots and lighting until eventually breaking out in tears and telling him to just forget it. Now Andy has become a curvy body expert, a title he carries with pride, as he anticipates my self-criticism and patiently takes the required eight hundred shots until I feel like my legs are less "globby," and my hair feels less "ugh" and "blah."

I put the bikini photos online, anticipating not only the cheers and support, but also the petty gossip and body bashing. I received both, and considered it a success. The story ran on both my blog and the *Huffington Post,* and a few days later as we drove down to Florida to visit Andy's parents who relocated there, I started to receive calls from the early morning network shows and afternoon talk shows wanting to interview me about daring to wear a two-piece bathing suit on the Internet.

Good Morning America sent a camera crew and producers to the house we were renting, and as the three cameramen set up lighting and adjusted shots, Jude walked up to the producer sitting beside me on the couch.

"Why's my mommy famous?" he asked.

"Because she wore a bathing suit." He tilted his head at him matter-of-factly.

"I do that all the time," Jude answered.

So did I. In fact, most people wear a bathing suit all the time, weather or season permitting. The difference was that most people weren't also fat and on the front page of the *Huffington Post* because of it. Everyone was so incredibly kind, but being interviewed about why as a woman I struggled wearing a bathing suit, by a male producer surrounded by three cameramen, was awkward. They didn't get it. Why is it difficult to be a curvy woman and wear a bathing suit? That's a really good question: why is it, society?

The segment was packaged and run alongside news that H&M had decided to use an attractive plus-size model for their swim line. And the tone of the story became less about how amazing it was that fat women were wearing bikinis and more focused on how dare they.

Sometimes, the biggest stumbling block to the cause of body positivity is traditional news media. While the Internet had exploded into a utopia of self-love and body acceptance, television and print media were lagging behind, like your grandma who still uses words like *coloreds* at your family Christmas dinner. For traditional media, fat women are only newsworthy when we hate ourselves or our existence is a caricature or oddity.

> *Plus-Size Woman Runs for Political Office*
>> *Obese Doctor Cures Cancer*
>> *Fatty Wears Bikini on the Internet*

The problem is that being 65 percent of the population, we aren't anomalies anymore; we're the majority. Here's an example of a real email exchange with a popular network morning talk show.

> To: Brittany
>
> From: Popular Network Morning Show
>
> Hello Brittany- Next week is Body Image week here at Popular Network Morning Show, and we'd love to have you on, are you interested?
>
> From: Brittany
>
> To: Popular Network Morning Show
>
> What a great theme, I'd love to participate; can you give me more details?
>
> To: Brittany
>
> From: Popular Network Morning Show
>
> Sure, we're doing a segment featuring plus size women sizes 8-12 who aren't happy with their bodies, and we'd like to have you come and talk about what parts of your body you aren't happy about.

To: Popular Network Morning Show
From: Brittany
Well, for starters I am actually a size 16, I'm not sure that
I'd quantify a size 8 as plus size? Also, I'm really happy
in my body. Wouldn't that be a much more positive
message to share during Body Image Week?

To: Brittany
From: Popular Network Morning Show
Sounds great, we'll call you within the hour to set
something up!

I'm still waiting for that call, and I have a feeling it won't be coming. We can't depend on the news to give us the talking points and narratives about how we're supposed to be feeling about our bodies. We need the women who are putting themselves out there in the bathing suits with the loud voices saying *look at me, this is what normal looks like, and it's beautiful.*

I am grateful every day that being one of those women gets to be my job. I've stopped cringing when someone at my kids' school asks me what I do for a living. I no longer write "Stay at Home Mom" on the blank line of emergency medical forms when they ask for my occupation because it's just easier than saying I take my clothes off in public. Now I write words like "advocate," "author," or "social media personality." Some people hit twenty and know exactly what they want to do with their lives; for me, it took another decade. Ten more years of being ashamed and unimportant and dragging along the self-esteem rock bottom in order to give me the strength, knowledge, and desperate drive to change *everything.*

15

THE TED TALK

IN 2011 I received an email from the organizers of TEDx, which is an offshoot of the popular TED Conference, *TED* standing for Technology, Entertainment, and Design. The event features eighteen-minute talks from a variety of sources, most of them being people who invent the Internet, cure diseases, or at some point were president. For a certified TED nerd, an invitation to speak is about as close to heaven as it gets, but at the same time, absolutely terrifying.

While they informed me I had been nominated to speak, the bigger question was, about what? What could I possibly say that was on par with the Brené Browns and Bill Gateses of the world? I responded to the email with an idea I'd had about how my life had changed after standing in Times Square in my bathing suit. It was superficial and lighthearted, and I fully expected an email response informing me all remaining spots had been filled and thanking me for my time.

Instead they said yes.

The event was held at Bowling Green State University, a college I did not attend, but had been drunk at many times. I showed up to the rehearsal dinner underdressed and late. Not because I wasn't punctual; I'd just spent too much time throwing up in the bushes next to where I parked my car. Skyler Rogers, the amazing man organizing the event, walked me through the process. I had eighteen minutes to speak, I was allowed no notes, and I was sandwiched between two guys who created animated robots for Disney and a guy who ended genocide or something. I'm honestly not sure what that second guy did; I was too busy hearing my own heartbeat in my ears to listen to that.

How do you compete with two dudes who make actual robots and somebody who probably ends the murder of innocent people? By talking about how I like myself in a bathing suit? That was my grand contribution to society? I felt physically ill, again. On the car ride home after the rehearsal, I asked Andy if it would be okay to back out.

"I'll tell them we have an emergency or I have food poisoning," I decided from the passenger seat of our car.

"You can't back out," Andy replied.

"Is it horrible to pray for sepsis?" I asked.

"You will be amazing."

"Or this could be the most humiliating experience of my life."

"That's unlikely. Nothing could beat you slipping into the grave hole at my grandma's funeral."

"They should mark those better," I sighed.

I can't remember when I fell asleep that night, but I awoke at 5:45 A.M. the next day with a strange peace washing over me. I had accepted my fate. The announcements had gone out, the programs had been printed, and the tickets had been purchased. Even if I sucked, even if I walked off the stage and left people thinking, *Why did they pick her to speak, again?* Even if no one clapped or laughed and every one shifted uncomfortably in their seats and checked their watches eight hundred times, this was happening.

I was in the second group of speakers, and as they pulled us to get miked before lunch, I made a life decision.

"I need you to tape this mike to my face," I told the young man attaching the Britney Spears headset to my ear.

"Huh?" he asked, staring at me confused.

"I need you to tape this mike to my face, because I don't want it to come off if I take my clothes off, okay?" I whispered.

"I-um," he stammered, unsure how to respond until he finally embraced the fact that I was probably crazy and he was on board with that. "Let me find some tape."

We worked in tandem and secretly backstage securing the headset to my cheek, hiding the tape with my hair. I might not have invented robots, but I could stand up there with my clothes off in the name of every woman who had ever hated her body. I stood on the side of the stage waiting for my intro, shifting uncomfortably in the bathing suit I'd hidden under my clothes. When Skyler beamed at me from across the stage and pointed at me to walk out, everything went bright white and silent.

I turned thirty and I became a swimsuit model.

The auditorium was a sold-out crowd of over six hundred people, mostly men in suits and college students who were looking at me with smirks on their faces.

I spent my first years of college as a bulimic. And the last decade or so coming to terms with how I really look. I've learned to like my body. It's just other people that seemed to have a problem with it.

Much like the way people scoff when you tell them you are fat and a swimsuit model, they have an equally hard time swallowing that you can be overweight and have an eating disorder. When you think about bulimia, you picture a bone-thin girl hovering over a toilet.

What you don't picture is a chubby college freshman on her

knees in the bathroom while everyone else is asleep, dragging her bloodied knuckles through the sweaty hair that stuck to her face, throwing up the last bit of food she'd binged on in her dorm room because she was always so hungry, but never wanted to face the consequences of the food she was eating.

I needed to change the way women saw their bodies. Magazines, ads, online, any of the five different Kardashian shows on E! . . . none of those women looked like me. I couldn't relate to their message and I couldn't relate to their lives.

We pay money every day to be reassured we aren't meeting the current standard of beauty. We not only are told that we're not good enough: we willing pay for the experience.

Because talking about change isn't as effective as being the change. So, that's what I had to do. I had to be the change I wanted to see. I had to redefine normal and beauty in this country.

And with that, I slipped off my shoes and unzipped my pants, leaving the crowd shifting in their seats, unsure if something poignant was about to happen, or I had the stage presence of Al Bundy.

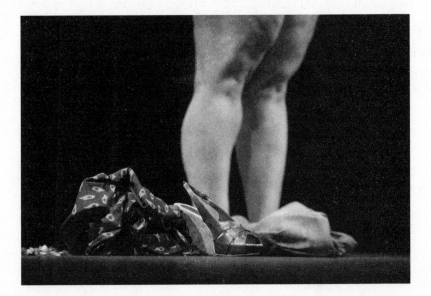

I stood, with five of my friends, in the middle of Times Square in New York City, on Good Morning America, between Emeril Lagasse and a cart selling hot nuts . . . in my bathing suit.

I looked at Skyler gripping his clipboard off the stage to the left. I stepped out of my jeans and pulled my shirt over my head.

I stood there to show people, I am what women in this country look like. There is nothing shameful or ugly about me. I can be confident and desirable at this size. I'm someone's mother, hell I'm three someones' mother, and I've earned every curve on my body. And I'll be damned if they aren't sexy.

My thighs rubbed as I crossed the stage. The bright lights that blinded me to the audience below afforded me a sense of safety and cockiness. I wasn't concerned about sucking in or showing my good side. I was just telling my story to a silent room of spotlights.

Was it worth it, standing there, every flaw exposed on national television? I don't know; how many of you have ever hated your bodies? How many of you untag yourself from Facebook photos, have been asked when you are due when you aren't even expecting, or gotten passed over by a guy for your thinner friend?

I've been all those people. None of them is less humiliating than the others.

I did this for you and for my daughter. And your daughter, and your mother and your friends. If you can get up in the morning and hate your body less than you did the day before, then it was worth every second next to that Hot Nut Cart.

I don't know how long I spoke. (It was eight minutes)

I can't remember anyone's face. (Except Skyler's when I started taking my clothes off. He was horrified.)

I don't remember the music I walked onto the stage to, but I'd like to think it was "Murder Was the Case" by Snoop. (It was "You Ain't Seen Nothing Yet" by Bachman Turner Overdrive.)

I ended my talk with a thank-you and instinctively grabbed my clothes from the floor and ran offstage into the bathroom.

The feeling was indescribable. It was more electric than climaxing or jumping into a pool of cold water. When I reemerged from the restroom and made my way out to the auditorium at intermission, I found a line of women waiting to speak to me, some of them crying, and men in line just to shake my hand. When I finally found my seat next to Andy, his eyes were shiny and he smiled. He told me I'd received a standing ovation, and next to giving him children, it's the proudest he'd ever looked at me.

It's been three years, and I still haven't been able to watch the video of my TED talk. In my head, it went perfectly, and I'd hate to ruin it by picking myself apart or focusing on anything other than the feeling I'd left the stage with that day: pure, unadulterated joy. That talk changed my life. It was the first time I'd addressed a crowd live, and despite being incredibly scared, I survived. Nothing would be as scary as that, which meant I could do anything.

I encourage you to watch the talk online; there's way more stripping that way. And I'd like to add that this speech has since been featured on the *Huffington Post* and Upworthy and by Meghan McCain, who called me her personal hero. And I'm only writing that right now because my dad is reading this, and it makes the Obama vein on his forehead stick out.

16

SEX WITH FAT GIRLS

May 22, 2012

To: Andy

From: Brittany

Hey, could you list 5 things you love about my body?

To: Brittany

From: Andy

Butt hair face lips cleavage.

To: Andy

From: Brittany

Whoa, slow down there Casanova, I'm about to end up pregnant, don't get so descriptive.

To: Brittany

From: Andy

Well, to be honest, I haven't seen you totally naked in years.

Well, shit. The fact is that even before kids, I was horrible at intimacy. The sex part was pretty basic, you put it in the hole, but the actual connection was where I struggled. The connection that kept me in the moment and enjoying the experience instead of focusing on what my body was doing and how it looked doing it. Plus, I come from a family of nonhuggers and I spend a good portion of my day hyperaware of my body, so yeah, recipe for Temple Grandin hug machine. My husband is gorgeous and very sexy, but the issues I was having with being naked and having sex were all me. Because I wasn't able to shut off my insecurities about my body and weight, sex had become a really anxiety-inducing experience that went one of two ways.

1   I avoided it because it was hot and stressful hiding naked under two comforters and a snowsuit in the dark, and instead would run a diversion play. *I have cramps. I have to work. I promised Gigi she could sleep in our bed.* That's right; I used a four-year-old as a cockblock.

2   I tried to explain to him why I was self-conscious, and then he asked why telling me how pretty I was wasn't enough for me to get over it, and I felt like a horrible, horrible asshole.

Becoming a mother, specifically the physical act of becoming a mother, totally changed my body by way of about fifty pounds. And while I'm on the topic of awkward ways in which sex is related to motherhood, we learn about relationships from our parents. The good, the bad, and the *oh my God promise me we won't be like them ever.* My kids were learning the dynamics of a relationship from two people who barely touched and lived like roommates. I'm not saying I want them to watch us make out or force them to watch our sex tapes. But there is a certain level of relationship confidence taught when one of the parents isn't hiding her naked body behind bathroom doors and jumping out of the arms of the man who loves her because her stomach is too flabby. If I couldn't be naked around Andy, the man legally obligated to love me, even after having watched three people climb out of me, who could I trust?

I had hit Pause on our relationship, and had been using life commitments and responsibilities as excuses not to hit Play again. As the effects of that grew, I got really worried Andy was losing interest because I was acting uninterested out of insecurity. Here I was spouting off about body love and wearing bikinis and buying pretty clothes, and at the end of the day, I wouldn't let him see me completely nude. When I was afraid to be seen in a bathing suit, I forced myself to wear one. When I was terrified to speak to a live audience, I climbed onstage. I conquer fears by making myself face them head-on, so if I was anxious about taking my clothes off, the natural remedy to that would be to strip. Unfortunately, I'm a horrible dancer and poles always leave a weird metallic smell on my hands. That only left two places I could face my nude body: the shower or the bedroom.

Standing in the shower until I was confident naked was a terrible idea, especially since we only have about twenty good minutes of warm water, and I'd get out of the shower days later freezing and looking like the old lady at the end of *Titanic*. That leaves sex.

I asked Andy if he'd be willing to have sex with me every day for one year in an attempt to help me get comfortable without my clothes on, barring any medical emergencies or logistical issues. And by logistical I mean travel, not anal, which I am surprisingly fine with. He said yes.

Our year started off pretty rough. I didn't realize how much time it took to prepare for sex, like shaving my legs in the sink and trying to make my hair appear messy-cute and not messy-homeless. Considering most of my romantic activities were rare moments of panties-pulled-to-the-side sex in a closet while the kids were napping, all this primping and prep work was reminding me why it was so much easier to just not put in the effort. We were tired, we had to be up early, and this project was quickly becoming just another chore to tack on to the end of our day, like taking my contacts out. I could fumble around with the case and solution, or I could just climb into bed and play pink-eye Russian roulette. Spoiler alert: I look adorable in eye patches.

The first three months, I didn't take my tank top off. After three kids and weight losses and gains, my boobs felt long and saggy. Bras were the only things making them still appear boob-shaped, and lying down without one left my nipples to pool down into my armpits. I was surprisingly insecure about this, so tank top with shelf bras became my security blanket.

We also had to address the monthly issue of my period. We could table the experiment for three to five days each month, or we could suck it up and get down with period sex. Surprisingly, every time I talk about this project with other people, the first question everyone asks me is what we did while I was on my period. The answer is we had sex. I think I was grossed out by sex during menstruation for about three seconds, then I remembered I've put way worse things in my body than some blood coming out. We tried having period sex in the shower for easy cleanup, but that is really hard unless you are the same height and once you accidentally get soap in your eye or inside your vagina, forget it. So for a few days every month, we put a towel down.

Around month six, we hit a turning point. I was in Los Angeles for a week taping a pilot for *Have Boobs Will Travel*, a fun travel show I was hired to host with Greg Grunberg, Alice Clayton and Keili Lefkovitz, and when I walked into my hotel just before midnight, exhausted from a day of shooting in Venice Beach, I found Andy there waiting for me. He flew across the country because he missed me. Not because I wasn't there to take care of the kids (note: who the hell is watching our kids?) or show him how to work the Keurig, but because he profoundly missed having me beside him in bed each night. And, surprisingly, I felt the same exact way. Going to bed without having sex with him made things feel incomplete and unfinished. Somewhere along the line, sex had stopped being an obligation and instead became the moment of the day I was the most comfortable and relaxed, the moment I could finally, *finally*, take my clothes off. And I did, all over that hotel room.

"What is it about hotel sex that's so hot?" he asked, naked and sprawled out across the messy bed playing with my hair.

"I think it's because the bedding is still white, we aren't paying the electricity bill so we can drop down to sixty degrees in here, and we don't have to clean any of this up," I said, gesturing around the now-messy room.

"Well, you have to clean that up." He pointed to the table covered in open lubes and sex toys he'd smuggled inside socks inside his carry-on. If I ever forget Andy loves me, I'll remember the time he went through airport security with a bag of anal plugs hidden in his socks.

Sex got easier after L.A. I took my tank tops off before climbing into bed, and I stopped methodically shutting off the lights and pulling a comforter over me. I even walked to the bathroom after we were done and peed naked with the door open. It wasn't always convenient, and it wasn't always even pretty, but the intention and desire for naked intimacy was there. I can't speak for Andy because this isn't his book and my voice is way higher than his, but I can assume he had a really good time having sex with his wife, again. On a personal level, it was an amazingly selfish year of using one of life's most intimate acts to take control of the way I viewed my body as a woman. This is what I've learned.

It's not you, it's me. Stop being weird about it.

I disliked my stomach. My thighs. How I looked lying flat on my back. A myriad of things, really, and I'd have the same conversation with Andy about it, telling him I'm self-conscious and I just don't feel sexy, and then he'd spend ten minutes telling me how gorgeous I am, and then another thirty pouting and being hurt that it wasn't enough to make me change my mind. So on top of feeling insecure, I felt like a jerk. That vicious cycle needed to stop. I needed to explain to him that seeing me that way is great, but unless I saw what he saw, too, it didn't count. I mean, at least if he expected me to be an active participant and not just a hole lying on the mattress.

It took a lot of talking to make him realize that me not feeling sexy was not an attack on him, and that him being hurt about it only made me feel worse. I wanted to enjoy sex, too. And the key for me being able to enjoy it is feeling confident and gorgeous, and that was a *me* journey, not a *him* journey, though having a cheerleader on the sidelines was a plus. We quickly learned that confident Brittany sex is way better, and there's way less crying.

Pretty panties make me happy.

I found that when I was at home in mom mode, I was opting for ease. And that's fine. I am not some bitch here telling you to wear heels to the grocery store or pants to pick up your kid at school when you aren't even getting out of the car and it's a total waste of clean pants. But one day I was getting dressed for an outside bridal shower in ninety-degree heat, and decided to forgo shapewear for regular underwear, when I realized the only underwear I owned was either ratty maternity underwear or cheap ninety-nine-cent briefs I grabbed at the end of a Walmart aisle to get me through my period week. No wonder I didn't feel sexy. I had the undergarments of an incontinent nursing home patient.

So I went to a department store and stocked up on adult woman underpants. Some were plain and some were lacy, and when I wore them they looked so pretty across my hips. I'd even find myself walking from my closet to the bathroom wearing them, a stark contrast to the primal run I did covered in a towel and with my Spanx shoved into a ball of clothes in my hands when I thought Andy wasn't paying attention.

I am my own sex advocate.
I like being on my knees and I don't climax with penetration, I only climax clitorally. I do like oral sex, but I don't like having my nipples touched, because they are numb. I also hate having breath on my neck because I am extremely ticklish, and then I get goose bumps and my leg hair grows in too fast. Please stop doing that.

I had to work on being okay saying all of that out loud, and get over the idea that I was being selfish and demanding. I deserve good sex as much as he does, and instead of waiting around for him to figure it out, which is totally unfair to guys, by the way, I had to find my voice and use it. Coincidentally, it was a major turn-on. Who knew?

If you think it's just about sex, then you aren't paying attention.
Going in, I knew writing about this project would be met with a certain level of voyeurism and cynicism. *Really, every*

day for a year? But what about your period? Isn't marriage about more than just sex? No, seriously, what happened when you were on your period? What I didn't expect was the instant viral explosion that occurred after I hit Publish. The story was picked up on the front pages of CNN, the *Huffington Post*, the British *Daily Mail*, and AOL. While this certainly wasn't the first time I received national news coverage for my body journey, it was definitely the first time it included insertion.

Woman Has Sex with Her Husband for a Year and Likes It!

Couple Has Sex Every Day for a Year,
Who's Watching the Kids?

Brittany Gibbons Is a Nymphomaniac, Is Hillary Clinton
Making a Run in 2016?

Within a week of publishing the article, the *Today* show flew me in to New York to be interviewed by Savannah Guthrie about my yearlong project, and I went because I felt like this was an important conversation. I wanted to talk about ways we, as women, can take responsibility for our self-esteem. Having sex every day wasn't meant to be seedy or scandalous; it was empowering. Unfortunately, none of that came across in the interview. Instead of asking why, I was asked how. How did I do this with three kids? How was I not too exhausted? How did I pull this off? How did I even walk after that much sex?

The ironic part was that the one time I finally wanted to talk about my body as the focus of the article, nobody wanted to ask me about it. For years the question had been "how did you find the confidence in your plus-size body to do this," and now all anyone wanted to talk about was what we did while I was on my period.

Shortly after the *Today* interview, Andy and I flew to Mexico with friends for a much-needed getaway. I mean, we'd just had sex for a year, and our genitals wanted to relax off the grid on a beach somewhere. After an evening of drinking and dancing in Playa del Carmen, Andy and I collapsed into our bed at our hotel and fell asleep almost immediately. Sometime after midnight, my phone rang.

"Buenos noches," I mumbled into my phone, in the half-Spanish, half-English dialect I'd become accustomed to over the week, clumsily slipping between the two to order drinks and thank servers for their work.

"Brittany, it's Greis. Turn on Jay Leno because he is talking about you in his monologue right now!" she squealed into the phone.

I sat up, instantly awake and sober, scrounging for the laptop I'd tossed in the suitcase in the name of relaxation and no deadlines. Some people might find it humiliating that Jay leno made fun of their sex life on national television (two nights in a row), but I found it to be hilarious, which says a lot, because Jay Leno is anything but hilarious these days, especially now that he's officially retired.

My sex life left the confines of PG-rated morning news and became nighttime fodder, teased about in late-show monologues and discussed on HLN's *Showbiz Tonight*. It wasn't that I didn't like that all of this was happening, though it did make Andy's job a little awkward—but hey, there are worse things you could be famous for than having sex with your wife. Still, a part of me was sad that once again the victory of a fat girl was lost to a mess of sound bites and shocking headlines.

Months later, after the buzz died down and our children were getting ample indoctrination into the loving relationship that was now mom + dad= 4ever, I awoke in bed and reached for Andy, but he's already left for work for the day.

August 5, 2013

To: Andy

From: Brittany

Alright man take two, five things you love about my body.

To: Brittany

From: Andy

Only 5? I'd pick the curve of your waist between your boobs and your butt, the spot on your wrist where you dab perfume, your hair when you take it down in the morning, the really soft skin between your boobs, and all the freckles on your arms and shoulders.

To: Andy

From: Brittany

Weird, those are my 5 favorite things, too. We have similar tastes in body parts; I should show you my freezer collection sometime.

17

THE EMAILS

Subject: How much I love you!

From: Brittany

To: Andy

I love you so much, sometimes it hurts my bones. I love you so much, I often forget what I was even doing. Like, I went to go to the bathroom, and then thought about how much I love you, then I walked back out and peed in my jeans. I love you so much air seems stupid compared to you. I love you so much that if you accidentally broke my new camera and shattered my lens because you set it on the car hood while you got distracted, I wouldn't even be mad at you because my love for you makes that physically impossible.

Now, say it back.

From: Andy

To: Brittany

Wait what?

From: Brittany

To: Andy

SAY IT BACK!!!!

In high school, my grandmother bought me the book *Letters to Sartre*, by Simone de Beauvoir. The book featured love letters between de Beauvoir herself to Jean-Paul Sartre, the famed French novelist, philosopher, and political activist, giving you an inside glimpse at their love and relationship, which was both stormy and addictingly passionate. It remains one of my favorite books to this day. You hear lots of people mourn for the lost art of writing letters, and I would be one of those letter-writing people if my hand weren't hardened into a giant texting-induced claw, unable to hold early-twentieth-century writing instruments. I do, however, mourn the loss of messy love. The kind of love that is spilling down the front of you as you struggle with both hands to hold on to it.

I never wrote Andy any letters. I actually don't even own stamps and haven't been inside a post office since 1995. Are they fourteen dollars now? I honestly have no idea?.

But I do pride myself on the power of the typed word, and use it often to convey emotion, complain about my lost airline baggage on Twitter, and write love notes to my husband. Like Sartre would have done, Andy saved all my emails. I'd like to think it was out of love, but he said it had more to do with potentially needing them as evidence one day. Love. It makes you crazy.

Subject: Sex Dolls

From: Brittany

To: Andy

Do you know anyone who can make a full body mold of me and all my holes?

From: Andy

To: Brittany

Your holes?

From: Brittany

To: Andy

Yeah. Ears, nose, mouth, belly button, butt, pee and sex.

From: Andy

To: Brittany

Sex hole, awesome, let's start the argument now, what's the goal here?

From: Brittany

To: Andy

Um- to make life size sex dolls to sell on the Internet? I saw on My Strange Addiction that gently used ones start at 6k on Craigslist.

From: Andy

To: Brittany

What does gently used mean?

From: Brittany

To: Andy

I think it just means she only gave head but still has her doll hymen, so maybe don't kiss her on the mouth?

From: Andy

To: Brittany

Some days the way your brain works makes me not want to kiss YOU on the mouth.

Subject: The Salon?

From: Andy

To: Brittany

Hey- what is this $100 salon charge every few weeks?

From: Brittany

To: Andy

Waxer.

From: Andy

To: Brittany

That seems expensive for waxing?

From: Brittany

To: Andy

It's a normal price, plus we can write it off as a medical expense.

From: Andy

To: Brittany

How is you being hairy a medical expense?

From: Brittany

To: Andy

I stopped going to my OBGYN because she always makes me get on the scale and I hate that, so I just have Rachel peek up there every 6 weeks to make sure it looks normal and cancer-free.

From: Andy

To: Brittany

But she's not a doctor?

From: Brittany

To: Andy

Who really is these days?

From: Andy

To: Brittany

Actual doctors?

Subject: The Pacific Time Zone Is Weird

From: Brittany

To: Andy

Greetings from the past.

From: Andy

To: Brittany

Not explaining this to you again.

from: Brittany

To: Andy

Anything you want me to change for you?

From: Andy

To: Brittany

Not how time zones work.

From: Brittany

To: Andy

I can do anything but be seen by your dad, for fear he might fall in love with me and cause a paradox that would result in your non-existence.

From: Andy

To: Brittany

You aren't in Back to the Future.

From: Brittany

To: Andy

We could rig the lottery!

From: Andy

To: Brittany

Nope.

From: Brittany

to: Andy

If you find out Danity Kane is getting back together, call me, I want to make sure to be ready for it.

Subject: Golf

To: Brittany

From: Andy

Hey- I'm going golfing after work, but it doesn't mean I want a divorce or that we need counseling. This is only a heads up.

To: Andy

From: Brittany

???

To: Brittany

From: Andy

I saw you talking about starting your period on Facebook this week, so I decided to play the offense. I'll bring home cake.

To: Andy

From: Brittany

We're soul mates.

Subject: Shopping List

From: Andy

To: Brittany

What am I getting on the way home?

From: Brittany

To: Andy

Children's Mucinex Cough, Advil for me, tampons if you can, and pop.

From: Andy

To: Brittany

What kind?

From: Brittany

To: Andy

Diet Pepsi.

From: Andy

To: Brittany

No, the tampons?

From: Brittany

To: Andy

OH! HAPPY CLAP I LOVE YOU, Ok Kotex Super- they're black.

From: Andy

To: Brittany

That's a good idea actually so you don't see how gooped up and slimy they get.

From: Brittany

To: Andy

The box. I mean the box is black. But I should invent those! I can make them green and call them Zombie Fingers!

From: Andy

To: Brittany

Too far.

Subject: Phantom Fetus

From: Brittany

To: Andy

I just felt something kick me from inside my stomach.
I assume it's one of three things . . . a parasite, the
Chipotle I had for lunch, or a fetus.

From: Andy

To: Brittany

Well for your sake, I hope you are full of tapeworms,
gassy or your email was hacked.

From: Brittany

To: Andy

#andyhatesbabies

From: Andy

To: Brittany

Stop hashtagging our emails.

From: Brittany

To: Andy

#andylikesbuttworms

From: Andy

To: Brittany

How are you classified as an adult?

From: Brittany

To: Andy

#andymarrieschildren

Subject: Flu Shot

From: Brittany

To: Andy

OMG.

From: Andy

To: Brittany

Here we go.

From: Brittany

To: Andy

You don't understand, I feel like my ears are underwater, and like, a mermaid is in them screaming.

From: Andy

To: Brittany

No.

From: Brittany

To: Andy

I just saw a duck in the bathroom covered in blood. It was the Bloody Mary of ducks.

From: Andy

To: Brittany

Last time I'm having this discussion. It was a flu shot, not tracker-jacker venom. Take a nap until I get home, you'll be fine.

From: Brittany

To: Andy

Tell that to Glimmer.

From: Andy

To: Brittany

No idea what that means.

Subject: My Birthday

To: Andy

From: Brittany

Hey, have you decided what you are going to get me for my birthday yet?

To: Brittany

From: Andy

Yep.

To: Andy

from: Brittany

Is it clothes? Because you probably don't realize this, because my sizing is really elusive, but I do most my shopping in Juniors. So, it really is best to not buy me clothes, because my frame is very unique.

To: Brittany

From: Andy

Right. It's not clothes.

To: Andy

From: Brittany

Is it jewelry, because it's hard for me to wear jewelry at work?

To: Brittany

From: Andy

And, by work, do you mean watching DVR'ed Cosby Shows and laughing at stuff you write on the Internet?

To: Andy

From: Brittany

Is my gift being insulted? Is this an early birthday present you are giving me right now? Because you totally already got me this for Christmas when you said my green beans tasted like a homeless man smells.

To: Brittany
From: Andy
It's not jewelry.

To: Andy
From: Brittany
Is it a dolphin?

To: Brittany
From: Andy
Did you want a dolphin?

To: Andy
From: Brittany
I don't want to ruin your gift or tell you what to buy me, but I'll tell you that if it's not a dolphin, I'll be disappointed.

Subject: Dishwasher Tabs
To: Brittany
From: Andy
Hey- I loaded the dishwasher but you're out of dishwasher tabs.

To: Andy
From: Brittany
You mean . . . WE'RE out of dish tabs?

To: Brittany
From: Andy
Yes, sorry. WE are out of dishwasher tabs, what kind should I get?

To: Andy

From: Brittany

The blue gel kind. And WE'RE also out of panty liners.

Subject: Memorial Day

From: Andy

To: Brittany

Hey- did you deposit those checks?

From: Brittany

To: Andy

Is that a joke?

From: Andy

to: Brittany

No?

From: Brittany

To: Andy

I doubt the bank is even open, Andy. It's the 14th anniversary of the Battle of Hogwarts. Do you know how many of my friends died in that war? It's insensitive for you to assume I'm even leaving the house today.

From: Andy

To: Brittany

So you're not going to the bank for me today then??

From: Brittany

To: Andy

I'm ashamed FOR you

18

WOMEN WE'RE RUINING EVERYTHING

"Obesity is NOT beautiful. Obesity is harmful and unhealthy. You made this choice. I am really tired of these big & beautiful articles."
—AURELIABELL, HUFFINGTON POST

"I'm just going to assume your husband is blind or lost a bet."
—JENNAV, BRITTANYHERSELF.COM

"You post pictures of yourself online so people will tell you you're pretty because nobody will say that to you in real life."
—KLM1984, BRITTANYHERSELF.COM

"Women like you should have your kids taken away. You can't grow up in life being okay with being fat. It's child abuse."
—DORY, YAHOO

"You aren't attractive; you're basically a fat fetish."
—BONNIE, CNN.COM

People are dicks to plus-size women. Moms equate your relationship status to your BMI. Aunts make passive-aggressive comments to you about what constitutes a girlish figure. The guy in line behind you at the Chinese buffet asks you if you're especially hungry that day. People walk around with a certain level of entitlement to your body, but it's nothing compared to the Internet. The Internet is a special place people can go to say all the extra-egregious things they are way too cowardly to say to your face.

Writing online has opened me up to an entire world of negative commentary. While it is, at times, soul crushing and obnoxious in a very *do you kiss your mother with that mouth* fashion, it's not entirely unexpected. I once saw commenters on a CNN.com article ridicule a blind paraplegic kid and then blame him for killings in Benghazi, so very little in terms of online discourse surprises me anymore. But what was unexpected was who it was coming from . . . other women. Men did it, too, sure, but the woman-on-woman genocide was a complete surprise.

In my personal experience, negative male commentary about my body is primarily full of superficial generalities, like "you're fat" or "you're ugly," further backed up by all the ways they wouldn't sleep with me, which would be devastating if my primary goals were making a man's dick hard. It's important to note, however, that the majority of online response I get from men is positive. They often applaud my curves, thank me for validating the bodies of their wives and daughters, and in some cases email me for my phone number and relationship status.

Women are a completely different monster. There is no greater species better crafted for emotional terrorism than women. We slice away at the Achilles until our victims are left feeling completely devoid of value and unfit for love, friendship, and in extreme cases, air. We've been bred to see others' successes as a direct assault to our own, and this is especially true when it comes to weight. Seeing someone who is heavier than us viewing themselves in a positive light is detrimental to our own self-esteem. So we attack and tear down until eventually that person feels as bad about herself as we do about ourselves. And for some reason, that goes into the win column. Hell, ladies, we don't even need the fashion industry and society to do this for us; we're busy enough trying to meet the demands of doing it to each other.

FAT SHAMING: YOU'RE DOING IT WRONG

A couple of things about fat shaming.

1 It's a real thing.
2 If someone says you are doing it, and your response is "am not," you probably are.

No one is arguing that obesity isn't an epidemic. We see it all over the news. Fat people with their heads cut off or blurred out walking down the street uncomfortably or eating in fast-food restaurants. Not the skinny people. The skinny people eating there are fine; it's the fat ones who are the problem. These are all images society needs us to see. We need to be told that this is what fat looks like, and *oh isn't it disgusting,* because I swear to God, that is the only way anyone can possible sleep at night or justify the way fat people are treated in this country

Reminding me I'm fat in the comments of my blog, bullying me in online forums, providing me with no fashion options, shaming me at restaurants, ridiculing me in gyms, mocking me on national television—how's that working out? Well, according to a recent study out of the Florida State University College of Medicine, not so great. "People who felt discriminated against because of their weight were more likely to become or stay obese." (That sound you hear right now is millions of plus-size people across the world sighing a collective "no shit.") I'm not trying to make anyone feel like less of a special snowflake here, but chances are, if you are calling somebody fat, you're probably not the first one to tell that person that. My guess is, it's been beaten into them the majority of their lives by several people before you. I'm not sure what the clinical trial time frame on shitty social experiments is, but we've been fat shaming people for years with an impressive zero percent success rate. Unless we're measuring success rates in suicides and eating disorders, in which case the numbers are slightly more impressive.

The reality is that fat shaming doesn't force me into being thin, and you can sit there from the comfort of your small pants and tell me I'm gross or unworthy of love until you're blue in the face, but it won't make me pick up a kettle ball. It will, however, make me pick up a candy bar in the closet where I hide to eat alone because seeing me eat in public grosses you out. That's right, motherfuckers, fat people adapt.

So how do I combat the shaming? Instinctively I want to grab the water bottle I use to squirt my cat with when she's being a dick, but based on the ineffectiveness demonstrated when I squirt my kids with it, it's probably futile. Also Andy kept screaming at me every time I sprayed his laptop with water.

Instead, I realized that people are allowed to say whatever they want to me about my weight, but it's entirely up to me how much power I let those words have over me. I'm not obligated or required to accept negative commentary about my looks. I'm not less confident or honest for ignoring that it's there. I'm just confident enough to know it's not true.

BUT THINK OF YOUR HEALTH

Are you a doctor? Are you my doctor? Am I shifting around uncomfortably on a paper-covered table in your house? No? Okay, then you don't get to make wild accusations about my health based on how I look because you are not a real doctor, you are a pretend Internet doctor. Not the same thing. You are basically as qualified to distribute medical advice as those douchebags from spring break who walk around with "Part Time Gynecologist" shirts on. As a rule, and you can decide how applicable you feel like this may be for yourself, I just go ahead and assume everyone is healthy unless they are actively mainlining heroin into their arms. It's a courtesy I afford all people by way of basic human decency.

After I had my second child, I was carrying the weight of two back-to-back pregnancies; literally, I had given birth twice in an eleven-month span, gaining a combined eighty pounds. While I physically felt okay, and my blood pressure and levels were all completely normal and healthy, I was mentally destroyed, living in my father's sweatpants and oversize men's T-shirts. I ran into an old classmate from high school in the grocery store and she asked me how far along I was. I was not pregnant. I woke up the next morning determined to lose weight.

I lived on a strict diet of 1,200 calories a day, and once my breast milk supply dried up due to lack of nutrients, I began bottle feeding, which freed up my ability to also incorporate drugstore weight loss supplements, 30 Day Shred, and random bouts of binging and purging. Within seven months I had lost close to ninety pounds and was wearing a size 12 jeans. My fingernails and toenails began to crack in half. My hair fell out, leaving quarter-size clumps around my hairline and scalp. I was acutely anemic, reliant on laxatives for bowel movements, experiencing tachycardia . . . and everyone told me I looked stunning. Truly, that I'd never looked better.

It's amazing to me that at my unhealthiest point, I was the most socially acceptable. Yet, here I stand today at 215 pounds, as healthy as can be, and a total abomination to society.

Some of the most offensive comments I receive are laced with concern over my health. I can forgive the attacks on my size or marital status because I write it off as ignorance and jealousy, but when they lubricate a stream of shame with backhanded concern for my health, it tells me that they are smart enough to know better, but choose to tear me down anyway.

"I'm not against fat people feeling good about themselves, you know, as long as they're healthy," said Caroline, on the *Huffington Post*.

Stop it. You don't get to legislate the parameters of my confidence. I get to feel good about myself because I am a person; my size has nothing to do with it.

IN DEFENSE OF REAL WOMEN

You can't throw a rock at the body acceptance movement and not hit a Marilyn Monroe picture.

"I see your clavicle and raise you Marilyn Monroe and Christina Hendricks. Boom. I just real-womaned the fuck out of you!"

Curvy women cling to her image, whipping it out like a cop badge at the first instance of fat shaming, ignoring the very real fact that Marilyn Monroe was not a plus-size woman, no matter how badly we wish it to be so. We foolishly stand there with our vintage photographs and Pinterest quotes, challenging thin women to a duel over what more clearly defines womanhood.

> *Real Men Love Curves*
>
> *Only Dogs Want Bones*
>
> *A woman without curves is like jeans without pockets; you don't know where to put your hands.*

A few years ago, I was all too eager to ride that train. In 2011, I created CurvyGirlGuide.com, an online magazine and community aimed at plus-size women. From its launch it took off as an undisputed success, winning awards hand over fist, landing contracts with fashion brands eager to cash in on the untapped plus-size market, and further perpetuating the mind-set that, finally, Real Women Have Curves.

It was an empowering message, and it gave women like me a feminine identity, something we'd been largely denied over the years. With companies like Dove stoking the fire, it all felt very okay and exciting. The skinny girls had had their chance in the sun, and it was their turn to be unmarketable afterthoughts for a while. Yes, *this* was winning. *This* was a movement. *This* was political. "Real" and "Curve" were now marketing mainstays.

Somewhere in the midst of all this empowerment and back-patting, another line had been drawn in the sand and history was repeating itself. We were once again presenting one body as the gold standard for beauty and womanhood, which is fun when you meet the requirements, but what about those who don't? Suddenly I had thin women reaching out to me, saying "what about us?" and "we hate out bodies, too!" It turns out fat women do not have the monopoly on body issues. I was running a website that spoke out against shaming, but at the same time I was sustaining a watered-down form of it.

That wasn't evolution; that was amnesia.

I always call myself an accidental advocate. I didn't intend to stumble into a job that had me on the front lines of the fight for body acceptance, but here I am. And as I stand at the top looking down, I realize this is not a plus-size movement, but a woman's movement. Strength and empowerment are not built on the backs of other women. The realness of a woman is not defined by her curves or lack thereof; real women are those who defend and empower all women, no matter what size their ass is. If we don't say enough and stop the race to the beauty-standard finish line, the casualties and the resentment women have toward each other will grow.

In 2013, I closed CurvyGirlGuide.com in its current form, and relaunched it as an interactive community, welcoming to women of all sizes. There are meet-ups and events attended by the thousands of members who call the sisterhood home.

NOW WHAT

If you were to ask me what the goal of this book was, I would tell you that it was to validate every student loan check my dad still has to write each month. And to tell the story of a woman who didn't have to lose weight to be great. To prove that those stories about chubby women who have it all aren't exceptions or television shows starring America Ferrera, but real life.

Feeling good in your skin is 80 percent mental. All right, I don't have the actual math on that, but 80 percent mental feels accurate, the other 20 percent being kick-ass shapewear and wine. The point is, you provide the narrative for how others perceive you. People treat me like a sexy and confident curvy woman because I act like a sexy and confident curvy woman; my behavior doesn't give them any other options.

I walk around knowing I have the right to never feel ashamed or disgusted with my body, and if people have a problem with it, it's on them.

"Hey, weirdo! Stop staring at my body. It's creepy."

EPILOGUE: NAKED

THERE IS NO better testament to the value of this book than the fact that I gained thirty pounds writing it. Normally I would make excuses for that statement, but the truth is, eating my way through writing this book for you was one of the greatest experiences of my life.

I could easily expand here with feel-good commentary about my body and why you should love yourself, but sometimes it's more meaningful to just shut up and show you already.

Thanks for buying my book. I can't wait to gain thirty more pounds while writing my next one.

ACKNOWLEDGMENTS

TK

ABOUT THE AUTHOR

TK